How to Live with Another Person

"Problems in living with another person become the central issue in too many lives," writes Dr. David Viscott. "People waste precious energy blindly trying to solve problems they don't really understand. As a result they may not have enough energy left to invest in becoming themselves. . . ."

In this vital handbook, Dr. Viscott stresses every person's basic right to grow, to be an individual, to be loved, to have privacy, to be trusted and respected, to defend oneself, to be accepted, to be happy, and to be free.

DAVID VISCOTT, M.D., is the bestselling author of *The Making of a Psychiatrist*, *The Language of Feelings*, *How to Live with Another Person*, *Risking*, *Taking Care of Business*, *Winning*, *The Viscott Method* and *Feel Free*, all available from Pocket Books. His latest, *I Love You, Let's Work It Out*, is available in hardcover from Simon & Schuster. Dr. Viscott hosts one of America's most popular syndicated radio talk shows, enjoyed by millions of listeners across the country, as well as the nationally televised "In Touch with David Viscott." Founder of the prestigious Viscott Institute, he lives in Los Angeles, California.

Books by David S. Viscott, M.D.

Feel Free
How to Live with Another Person
The Language of Feelings
The Making of a Psychiatrist
Risking
Taking Care of Business
The Viscott Method: A Revolutionary Program
   for Self-Analysis and Self-Understanding
Winning

Published by POCKET BOOKS

HOW TO
LIVE WITH
ANOTHER
PERSON

David Viscott, M.D.

POCKET BOOKS

New York   London   Toronto   Sydney   Tokyo   Singapore

POCKET BOOKS, a division of Simon & Schuster Inc.
1230 Avenue of the Americas, New York, NY 10020

ISBN: 0-671-73558-6

First Pocket Books printing February 1976

26   25   24   23   22   21   20   19

POCKET and colophon are registered trademarks of
Simon & Schuster Inc.

Printed in the U.S.A.

Until the nations and peoples of this world come to understand that nothing is more important than a human life and that all laws and governments should have as their goal the safety of the people and the prevention of the taking of the lives of innocents, we shall be forced to mourn the needless loss of our best, people who exemplify the noblest and highest aspirations of the human spirit itself.

JERRY WOHLBERG
(1939–1973)
Much Beloved

"Alas, how love can trifle with itself!"

Two Gentlemen of Verona, Act IV

CONTENTS

INTRODUCTION

I SUPPOSE everyone has to live with someone else at least once in his life. Much has been written about the psychology of individuals and groups. Many of today's psychological theories seem verified by experience and proved by experiment. However, our understanding of how two people interact over the course of a relationship has come to us mostly from novelists and from our own personal struggles with our close relationships, in which we try, as best we can, to find solutions to problems as we are able to see and meet them at the moment. It is an inexact undertaking and often painful and frustrating.

Each of us must prove our own theories about living with another person. How much better it would be if there were some easier way of knowing you were doing the wrong thing than to make a second mistake. Judging from the way the divorce rate in this country is rising, a lot of people have made at least one. Too many people destroy themselves through a relationship they do not know how to handle. Mismanaging a special relationship will at one time or another interfere with your ability to work or to concentrate on other matters or to feel good about yourself. This applies to anyone who has ever lived with another person and anyone who ever plans to. Problems in living with another person become the central issue in too many lives. People waste precious energy blindly trying to solve problems they really don't understand. As a result they may not have enough energy left to invest in becoming themselves and may hold their relationship to blame for their personal failure. It's harder to find personal success when you don't get along with the people you love. Even if that is only part of the problem, it's an important part.

Even though people seldom see more than they are ready to see and can't be forced to feel what they don't want to feel, there must be a way of looking at a relationship which enables both partners to live together more fully.

I don't claim to have all the answers here. I'm hardly perfect and don't always follow the answers I'm sure of. I'm not proposing a new school of psychology. I'd just like to think about living with another person and share my thoughts with you and see how far we go in understanding what happens when two people live together.

Chapter One

BETWEEN TWO PEOPLE

COME on, admit it.

You've been living with someone for a while now and you sometimes think you've made a mistake, a big mistake. There are things you want to do that you can't because the person you are living with gets in the way.

You feel cheated. You're missing a lot. You can't stand thinking about it because it hurts so much. Sometimes you just want to be alone, free to be and do whatever you want.

The point is that if you had the opportunity to do what you wanted you probably wouldn't because you really love and need this other person. And, as strong as is this force to explore, there is another force just as strong holding you back.

Still, a part of you is aching, going unanswered. Is the price of living with another person always so steep? Do you always have to give up a part of yourself that you need? Is it going to be like this forever, wanting what you want but not being able to have it?

Too many relationships are based on such childish, unrealistic ideas of possessing each other that it is difficult to grow and develop as an individual without hurting the other partner. Yet there must be a way to have a full, warm, loving relationship with another person and still be true to yourself, still leave room for personal growth and for keeping your rights as an individual—and still be your own person.

Today most people feel pressured by an unfriendly world. People tend to feel helpless and without direction. It is increasingly difficult for any person to feel good about himself.

The hectic pace of civilization has dulled our senses. Once people were more alert to everything around them. Now the world is overwhelming and we are forced to filter out so much noise and confusion that in the process we often distort much of what is important or miss it completely, and sadly we begin to act this way with the people we love.

Everywhere around us are objects of great size, buildings that block out the sun, cities that separate us from nature, and governments that seem large and impersonal. Our loves seem less and less our own and our destinies seem increasingly influenced by factors that are out of our control. People with special interests take advantage of others less fortunate than themselves.

In the face of these oppressive forces it sometimes seems impossible to find a sense of personal identity in the world that makes us feel strong. Perhaps there is little we can do to change the course of world events, but there is much that each of us can do to improve our private lives that would make us feel better as individuals.

To keep from going mad as our personal living space grows smaller, we must find ways to get along with each other that allow us to preserve our individuality, to make use of our talents and to grow and still make it possible to live with another person and enjoy the closeness and support that such a relationship offers.

Relationships seldom die because they suddenly have no life left in them. They wither slowly, either because people do not understand how much or what kind of upkeep, time, work, love and caring they require or because people are too lazy or afraid to try. A relationship is a living thing. It needs and benefits from the same attention to detail that an artist lavishes on his art.

Our special relationships should be places where we can be closer to ourselves and others, places where we can become more human, where our feelings become most real and where our sense of ourselves is strong.

The story of the relationship between two people is at once the most familiar and the most complex we know. It is as varied as it is involved and as rewarding as it can be trying.

We see the most accurate picture of ourselves reflected in the responses we arouse in another person we know well. Although we may be aware of our thoughts and feelings, we tend to hide them from others. Even though we wish we could share them and be more completely understood, the innermost parts of ourselves remain private. Our casual acquaintances really don't know us at all. Unless it is possible to open ourselves to another person and entrust him with the story of our past, our feelings about the present and secret hopes for the future, we are bound to remain lonely and, ironically, in a world which is becoming oppressively close, we will only begin to feel more isolated and shut off.

It is in the interface between ourselves and another person whom we share with and trust and with whom we are sometimes so close it is difficult to say where our feelings end and the other's begin that we are uniquely able to see ourselves to

be as good as we really are. This view we derive
of ourselves from another person is not always
easy to put into words. It is a feeling, a state of
being that says, I am good, I am worthwhile, I am
very important to another human being who is as
important to me.

Being each other's may define only part of any
person's identity, but the part that it defines, it
defines completely.

Another way to define ourselves as individuals, besides through a relationship with another person,
is to become so involved in the pursuit of our
work, art, career that we are able to control completely a little world of our own, a realm over
which we have influence, and to let the world outside go mad if it chooses to.

Each of us must become the artist who shapes
our own lives by creating a purpose and a life-
style to fit our view of ourselves, a way of life
that allows us to become the person we feel most
happy being. Rather than trying to change the
whole world, we need only to create a place in it
where we can fulfill ourselves, where we can find
a life shaped not by an indifferent world or by
chance, but by the depth of our talents and the
sincerity of our determination in developing our
gifts whatever they may be.

There are parts of ourselves each of us must discover alone, parts that no other person can share. There are moments when each of us must go it alone, when no one else can help. Even so, fulfilling our promise as an individual is an incomplete experience until we share our discovery with another human being and thereby are seen more completely.

The act of creation is such a moment. The artist shares his most private self with the rest of the world. His sharing is his gift. In the act of artistic creation, in giving form to thoughts and sensory images, the artist retells the history of the life force flowing through all living things. Few people can tolerate the long isolation of artistic creation or of any other lonely work without the support and understanding of another human being even if that creative work is self-fulfilling.

To give a gift freely one must feel given to.

To be a full human being one must be uniquely oneself and also another's.

Of all feelings, loneliness is the worst. To be lonely is to lack something that makes you feel complete. Sometimes it is another person. Sometimes it is a part of yourself you want desperately to know really exists, a higher view of yourself that gives your life meaning. Sharing our secret loneliness, even incompletely, is enough to make us feel less alone.

In sharing our hurts and vulnerabilities we develop trust. Learning to trust another person helps us overcome adversities which would make us feel hopeless if we faced them alone. Trust is the creation of two people who care for each other and believe in the relationship between them.

Sometimes we live in our own little world, created from the special part of ourselves that is uniquely ours.

Sometimes we share a place with another person. To discover who we really are we need both a place where we can apply our talent and discover ourselves and a relationship where we feel accepted and understood. But we should not expect a relationship to fulfill the same needs for individual expression that a career can, nor expect a career to provide the answer to one's loneliness that a relationship can.

And yet some people still try to build a relationship in their own image because they have not yet found themselves as individuals. They demand attention from their partner that is never the right kind or enough. Other people seek a sense of togetherness in their career or job and spend their lives trying to understand why their success leaves them feeling incomplete. Both approaches place unrealistic burdens, one on a relationship, the other on the self.

No relationship can reveal all parts of ourselves or make it unnecessary for us to risk ourselves in the world in search of our individual identity, just as no amount of self-fulfillment makes other people unnecessary.

Our needs must be filled by whatever creates them. We need food when we are hungry, we need love when we feel lonely and a sense of pride in our life when we feel worthless. In the best relationships people fulfill the need they create in other people.

It is unrealistic to think that great personal accomplishment or a life of fame and material fullness can ever fill the sense of emptiness that eats away at a person who doubts his own lovability. Some needs can only be fulfilled by another person. Some needs can be filled only by oneself. Knowing which is which and being willing to take the risk of making your needs known, admitting you are human and need another person as much as you need yourself is the first step on the way to becoming complete.

The problems of living with another person are not so difficult to understand or solve. What is needed is the desire to understand and to make the relationship work.

Never underestimate the effect one person can have on another. More important than a change in government, an unexpected inheritance or one's fortunes in the marketplace, one person can re-kindle a flame long thought dead and bring life where only cynicism formerly lived.

To love and be loved is to feel the sun from both sides.

Chapter Two

EVERYONE'S
BASIC RIGHTS

ANY relationship which does not respect the rights of its individual members equally cannot be based on an understanding that goes very deep. A relationship should be a place where each member regards the other's rights and feelings as he would his own.

Usually two people come to accept each other's rights by trial and error and by argument and misunderstanding. Each couple must decide for itself what is acceptable in its relationship. This may take years and involve periods of disenchantment, self-accusation and feelings of isolation and betrayal. The course of all relationships is occasionally stormy, even if the partners never seem to argue.

We are all human and that simple fact makes us heir to the noblest aspirations, the basest instincts, an attraction to what is beautiful, a potential for angry retaliation and the capacity for love and self-sacrifice.

29

We are each a story and no one's story is completed until his death, no matter how hopeless the opening chapters seem to be or how limited their future development appears. Neither is a happy outcome a certainty no matter how great and promising one's beginnings are. We are all becoming and none of us can be sure what it is he will finally become. The process from beginning to end is hard work. The times are always uncertain. Our greatest strength comes from protecting our rights.

We are all born with the same rights. These rights are ours whether we assert them or not, whether we live alone or with another person. Our rights are always the same. Our rights are natural rights, our claim to them is our life itself and our belief in equality, and the right to express and satisfy our rights always depends upon our respecting the rights of others. When we deny another's rights we only deny ourselves.

No one can force another person to give up his rights, even though one partner may overpower another and get his way for a time. The only person who can give up rights is the person who owns them. Such yielding should be only temporary and occur as part of the give and take in a relationship which naturally balances itself.

If we completely abandon our individual rights in favor of another person when we form a relationship, we only violate ourselves, become less of a person and in the end undermine the relationship itself. There is always a price for yielding rights. When we cede rights insincerely or are forced to yield them against our will, we often secretly hold the other person liable for our loss and for the pain that always comes from giving away a part of ourselves that we need in order to feel like a complete human being. Our pain comes partly from the discovery that we no longer feel true to ourselves and partly because we feel we have become less of a person through our relationship than we were before.

A long-held secret resentment over trampled rights becomes a silent negative force seeking expression. It can flow through a relationship, attach itself to trivial arguments, make small anger great, taint what is good and angrily leak out everywhere.

A person's individual rights in any relationship are the same rights he enjoyed before he even knew the other partner existed. Rights are not to be bargained for. They simply exist. A relationship's task is to recognize and protect the rights of both parties. It should allow two people with equal rights to live together so that both of them can grow and share a view of the world which is greater than either sees alone.

If two people living together do not generate a world that is greater than the sum of each of them alone, their union is superficial and static.

The Right To Grow

Both partners must allow each other the freedom to grow even if that freedom is a threat to the relationship. The freedom to grow up is also the freedom to grow apart. When one partner prevents the other from realizing his fullest potential he releases the most undermining force in the relationship. That partner is in effect saying to the other: You must always be the person I want you to be. You must always stay the same. Your purpose in life is what I see it to be. And your growth is a threat to me.

Trying to place restrictions on the growth of a partner is always a mistake and destined to fail. A relationship should be a place where two people share the experience of helping each other become more than they were when their relationship started. It should never become a jail, holding their souls hostage for a ransom of love which is conditional on their always staying the same. Such a relationship only dissolves when a partner discovers an unconditional love or learns how important it is to be himself.

To demand that a person stop growing is not to love the other person fully. You should love not only what the other is, but also what he can become.

Loving a person is to love the best in him and to make it easier for that person to become himself.

Any force that stands in the way of our becoming is alien to us. To have someone who shares your closest thoughts and feelings stand in your way is to be tripped on your own doorstep before you have had a chance to try your fortunes in the world. The worst thing one partner can say to the other is, "You kept me from being me."

You have a right to become the person you were destined to become. To feel that someone is blocking your destiny is one of the worst of all feelings. There are enough obstacles in the world that prevent people from fulfilling themselves without adding to them by demanding that a partner give up his plans for the sake of a relationship. Such demands only backfire and weaken the strong emotional ties between the two partners.

Even if it seems threatening at first, helping a partner grow and find himself always makes a relationship stronger. In time the partners will seem less dependent and less possessive. They remain together because they want to be together. Although they have the freedom on each day of the relationship's life to stay or to leave, they choose to stay and grow together. The strongest relationship is the one between two people who see each other as midwives to the persons they wish to become.

Any time one partner feels that a part of himself he loves must be kept secret in the presence of the other, the relationship is in serious trouble. The part that is held in secret demands to be expressed and, when an opportunity arises to grow in a way that promises to make this part free, the opportunity quickly becomes the wedge that splits the old relationship apart and loosens its ties.

The Right To Be Yourself

Every person has the right to be himself, the person he is, the sum total of his feelings, thoughts, affections, tastes, dislikes and perceptions.

What is it to be a person if it is not to see and feel a world that no one else sees or feels but you, to be a world unto yourself that exists only as long as you do?

Who sees your world or knows how the color of your sadness changes the sunsets? Who sees the part of you that smiles on yourself, that fills you

34

with love and makes the people in your world smile back?

We spend our lives existing between two worlds we can never really grasp and so we live in a world of our own creation. To avoid being hurt and to be comfortable, each of us perceives the world he must perceive. We invent our illusions to separate the world outside from the world within. Even though the outside world is the same and feelings are universal, no two people share the same illusion.

Nothing hurts us more than a wound that cuts through our illusions and makes us see the parts of ourselves we were unwilling to see before.

To live with another person is to try to share the world he perceives and in so doing to permit your world to grow and to give up your illusions through love.

How do we know the world each of us perceives is real? No person can be completely objective. Each of us can make out only part of the truth, the part that is similar to what each of us can accept in ourselves.

No matter what your view of the world is, it is yours. More than that, it is you. You have the right to be you, to say "I am" and to have that mean something very different from what anyone else in the world who says it means and still have it mean many of the same things.

No one has the right to make you change, but if you want to change, it is your right to do so. A relationship cannot continue to exist when one person demands that the other change in order to keep the relationship alive. A person doesn't really change unless he wants to.

The best kind of change can happen through the love of one person for another. When two people allow each other to get close enough to share the private corners of their worlds of feeling and thought, they develop a trust that allows each to see his own world anew through the eyes of the other person and so each partner learns to see himself in a new way. Because their perception of themselves changes, so do their worlds and so too do they. They change because they see a better them.

It is difficult to change when all you hear is someone telling you what is wrong with you and you suspect that there may be nothing better to be gained by changing. Why risk changing for the worse for someone if he can't see the parts of you that exist now that you already know are good? How sure can you be that the other person will like what you become if you change to please him? How sure are you that you will like yourself?

You are your feelings and thoughts, your actions and intentions. You have a right to feel whatever you feel, to be whoever you are.

Only when all memory of you fades is the right to be you yielded.

The Right To Be Loved

Without love nothing is right. A life without love is not right. A life without love is a world without love.

Every person has the right to be loved and to love
To be accepted, cared for and adored
And every person has the right to fulfill that right.

The right to love is the right to be intimate, to share, to be close, to know a mutuality of spirit based on acceptance of each other as you are.

To love a part of another that is not real is to hope the other will become someone or something that he is not.

We ought to love each other for what we are and for our potential for becoming.

Love is not our hope for another person, because that hope may only be a creature of our own creation, a wish for ourselves that we have been powerless to fulfill. Love can never be the burden of our hope for ourselves placed onto another person.

If we go on hoping we merely postpone the day when we can love another person completely for himself as he is.

Love is always now.
Even the memory of a love long past is now.
An old love never dies, it just exists in a quieter
place.

The Right to Privacy

The right to privacy, like most rights, reflects a simple human need. A life without privacy is unthinkable. Some people need more privacy than others, but everyone needs some time alone to be accountable only to oneself, time to think, to reconsider the things one believes and the reasons for those beliefs.

Privacy is the guardian of our incomplete thoughts, of our unconsidered opinions. Privacy is the force that takes the pressure of the moment and puts it aside, allowing the judgment of time to cast its relieving shadow over the present and help us fit our lives into the scheme of things.

No two people develop feelings or think or grow the same way. Protecting the right to privacy in any relationship is one way of insuring that each person can get his bearings and be himself.

People need a private life, a private world of their own, places where they can see friends, have conversations, maintain cherished interests, hobbies, amusements and sports, places where they can continue to be and find the other parts of the person they want to be and need to be, besides the parts that the person they are living with brings out.

The right to privacy is the right to spend time alone with yourself, but it is not the right to make other people worry unnecessarily about you by being thoughtless. Spending time alone should not be capricious or impulsive when other people are involved in your life. The right to privacy is the right to take a vacation alone, to spend some time alone with yourself each day, each week, each year.

Sometimes asserting one's right to privacy feels threatening to the other person. When relationships become frayed and at loose ends, partners have a way of regarding such requests for privacy as a wish to desert. Sometimes they are, but even then each person still has the right to be by himself to think the situation through alone. When the trust needed to keep a relationship working wears so thin that privacy is compromised, the relationship suffers doubly, for then it is not only difficult to be each other's but also a problem to be one's own.

You have a right to keep part of your life secret, any part. Your thoughts, actions and wishes are yours to keep private if you want. Not all thoughts need to be or should be shared. Openness in a relationship is a desirable goal but not in all things or at all times. Sometimes a partner needs more time to think before he shares. Being open indiscriminately can be an excuse to be cruel and to hurt the other person with information that is shared only as an act of anger.

Merely wishing to keep a thought secret should not suggest sinister intentions. Keeping a secret is merely a way of saying you are unsure of what you are feeling at the moment and do not wish to share it yet.

When there is no privacy in a relationship there can be no real intimacy. Only two people who are whole, independent beings in their own right can give to each other. Only if a person has the right to refuse to give is his gift worth taking. If one person is always obligated to be giving there is no delight for the person being given to.

If one has no right to privacy what joy is there in sharing?

The Right To Be Trusted

You have the right to be trusted until you give people reason to believe you are not worthy of their trust.

Trust is a living feeling.
It grows with a relationship.
It is fragile,
Very easily broken
And often irreparable.

Sometimes it takes years for two people to learn to trust each other.
And some people never trust the person they live with.
If you only trust people who do things that please you, there is no one you can trust.
If you trust everyone, you are a fool.
If you trust too soon, you are probably afraid of being rejected.
If you trust too superficially, you may easily be betrayed.

If you trust too late you may never know what
  love is.

To trust another is not to throw all cautions to
  the winds.
You must still look out for yourself.

Just because you trust one another does not mean
  that you will always do what is best for each
  other.
But it does mean you will try if you can.

To trust another person not only means that you
believe he will not hurt you intentionally, but that
you feel he will take your interests as his own and
so will avoid situations where he could hurt you
unintentionally. To trust each other is to be vulnerable in the same way.

The Right To Be Respected

You have the right to be respected so long as you
respect others. Respect cannot exist unless it is
mutual. If you don't respect yourself it is not
possible for you to respect another person's love
for you.

You have the right to be taken seriously. In fact
you must insist on being taken seriously. Which

does not mean that you must always be serious or without mirth.

You have the right to speak your mind and to be listened to. All of your opinions about your relationship should be as important to the other person as his own. Your ideas have equal importance in that forum even if nowhere else.

In order for a relationship between two people to work it must be a place where both of you are equals. You must be listened to by the other or else only half the truth is known. If only one person in a relationship needs to be taken seriously and listened to, it is not a relationship but a performer and an audience.

The Right of Acceptance

You have the right to be accepted as you accept others. You have the right to be tolerated even when you act foolish, childish, when you are afraid or are in pain. You have the right to be taken in when you need to be taken in.

You have the right to be wrong and to make good a mistake.

You have the right to have your apologies accepted, your thanks appreciated and your love cherished in the spirit it was given.

To accept another requires that you accept the part of yourself that the other brings out and that you not be ashamed of your own weaknesses.

To accept is to take the injured spirit of a friend like a mother receiving the arm of a child after a fall. When we accept someone we accept the sum of his parts. When we accept all of a person it does not mean that we accept everything he does, but it does mean that we will not reject all of him for the parts we do not accept.

The Right To Be Happy

No one really has the right to be happy just like that. No one has the right to a carefree and full life without losses or worries.

Only death is without care.

You have the right to seek happiness as you define it. You have the right to find yourself, to discover where your strengths are, to apply yourself, to seek the best opportunities for developing those strengths and to be judged by the work of your head and hands without prejudice.

To be happy means to become the person you want to be, to share your world with someone who loves you and to find your best work pleasing.

Only people who do not have these simple things want more than this. They are unhappy with themselves and try to solve the problm of their emptiness by demanding more from others outside themselves.

It is because of neither vanity nor greed that people mistakenly seek happiness in this way, but out of an attempt to escape from the parts of themselves they fear to face.

The Right To Be Free

Both parties to a relationship must be free. Neither party should play the role of guardian or caretaker to the other or presume to know what is best for him and insist that he be a certain way.

What each of you is to the other in a relationship you must be so freely. Two people should be together when they want to be together, not by schedule or decree.

To be free means that you are allowed to follow your feelings and the dictates of your heart and your good sense. There is no formula for making sure the other person will always respond to you in a certain way or will always love you. You can hope for the best if you allow your partner to be whatever it is he wishes to be, to love whatever parts of him you love without resenting him for the parts that you wish were there and to trust that he in turn will respond to you by allowing you to be whatever you want to be and accept you just as you are.

In a free relationship both partners always keep an option to walk out if and whenever they choose to. Both partners understand this fact and accept their shared vulnerability. In so doing they respect each other's feelings and assume the full consequences for their actions and statements. They are held together by an understanding, by a shared view of the world that allows each of them to be free and by a trust in each other's love.

There is no greater way of expressing love for another person than by allowing him to be whatever he is. When a relationship is really free and accepting both parties have little to fear, for nothing can compete with a free relationship.

The Right To Defend Yourself

You have the right to look out for yourself, to keep other people from taking what is yours, to stand up for your rights, to protect yourself in an argument, in an agreement or in any relationship you enter.

You have the obligation to see that your welfare is not sacrificed in the name of causes you do not believe in or for a relationship you mistrust.

You have the right to save yourself, to get up and walk out of any situation in which your best interests are being threatened. You have the right to protect yourself in any relationship so that you maintain your equality and keep from being used.

You have as much right to defend yourself as anyone has a right to attack you. And you have a right to exercise that right.

You have a right to believe in what you feel and what you know from your own experience. You must believe in yourself, devote your life to making yourself the best possible person you can be. No matter how the arguments for the opposition are disguised, be they in terms of money, patriotism or loyalty, no matter in whose name you are asked to betray your best self, never give in. You can never replace yourself.

If you will not defend your right to be you, who will? Who should?

Chapter Three

DEFINING A
RELATIONSHIP

IT IS not easy to say what defines a relationship. Each relationship is different because it is a world shared between two people. Every person is different and so is the world each couple defines.

Each of us lives in a private world which we furnish with images from our previous experience. The richness of that inner world depends upon the life we are exposed to and our receptivity to that exposure.

No two men ever died for the same country. While we may allow other people to enter and even live in our private world from time to time, and while we may reveal a part here, a corner there, the total reality, the inner world of our feelings remains largely inaccessible to others. If we are not islands unto ourselves, we are at best peninsulas.

Sometimes we join with another person and form an entirely new reality. There is a bond between some people neither time nor distance can erase.

It is a bond born out of a special shared kinship which cannot be expressed in words, but only felt.

Two people who mean a great deal to each other create a world that only exists when they are together. The time they share becomes their country and their thoughts about each other, their history. When they separate even for a short time they both become a little lost, like wanderers looking for a familiar face in a crowd or trying to identify shadows and footsteps in the distance. In time and with trust two people begin to accept the world of their creation as real and no longer worry about being apart because the other person lives inside them.

A relationship with another person is a place where you don't feel alone. It is a place where you can be a special part of yourself, where when something goes wrong another person cares as much as you to make things right again.

A relationship is a place to love. Loving is the most human of all acts. Through loving we cease to be alone and become part of mankind. Loving allows us to overlook faults common to everyone and to forgive and accept each other in spite of our shortcomings so that we are encouraged to grow.

To love is to care about the feelings of another person as you do about your own.

When you share something you love, you often find a new reason for loving what you have shared.

Everything you share in a relationship becomes both of yours and is not diminished for either. Sharing feelings is our natural imperative. We have no choice in the matter. Because we experience the world around us, we have feelings about it. Because we have feelings we must share them. Sharing feelings makes them more real. Sometimes saying "I feel" is the most convincing way of saying "I am."

Utopia is a place where it is easy to tell what is real from what is not.

The point of a relationship is to make both people as real as possible to each other.

The most important human experience is to be validated. To be validated is to have someone see the most secret part of you, the part you fear will be rejected if seen, the part you care about most, and to have that part shared and understood beyond the meaning of words. To be accepted for what you are means you can never be lonely for yourself again.

Sometimes the meaning of a relationship is only understood when it is over.

I

I walked by our old place
And found myself counting stones.
The ones I used to throw for luck,
Checking to see who'd been there
While we were gone.
It's funny how important a place becomes
How private
How easily intruded upon.
Our place was us and when that ceased to be
A part of my world became ordinary
Like stones.

II

Sometimes I look out across the land
And still sense winter in the spring.
I search for signs to reassure myself
That the worst is past,
But all I feel is the days seeming longer,
Empty without you.

One touch of you made winter fly
And fixed the world in spring.

The strength of a relationship comes from the constancy of affection and the dependability of the emotional support and understanding of each partner for the other, the love they share through time. The strength of a relationship is not determined by the religious ceremony that sanctified it, for the marriage agreement does not accurately describe the relationship in which it binds people together. Nor is it defined by any other agreement made at any other specific time.

The strength of a relationship is determined by the willingness of both parties to share their feelings and remain open to each other and by their ability to understand that each day both of them must learn to love a new person. No agreement holds a relationship together better than the understanding that a relationship is founded on honesty and growth and that the process of living itself redefines the relationship whenever the two interact.

Some people will want rules to define a relationship. There are no rules, only truths that must be uncovered and faced together.

People who form a relationship with another do not give up their rights to be themselves or to solve their individual needs.

Everyone has many facets and no single person can match all the facets or fill all the needs of another. The best we can hope for is to help fulfill each other where we can and not lament what is impossible or stand in the way of the fulfillment we cannot offer.

If two people could fulfill most of each other's needs completely, they would have little need for anyone else, at least for a while. But they should take care that what may have begun as the closest kind of sharing does not eventually become an invasion of the privacy of both partners.

Two people in a close relationship need space. With the world nowadays beginning to feel as if it is closing in on us, it is important that the most important relationship in our life allow for some kind of relief and not to insist on an unyielding togetherness which will only aggravate feelings of being trapped.

Any person, no matter how much beloved, how urgently desired or how hard fought for, can become an irritating source of conflict if he persists in invading our personal life space and doesn't give us room, especially when we need to be alone.

When our need for space in a relationship is ignored, it is a double injury because the person who invades our space is the very person we most expect to understand our need for room to live and breathe.

Each couple must make their own arrangements about private space, which should be mutually agreed upon and clear. The other person will not always understand your needs for space unless you make them known. Everyone needs to be told. Everyone must establish some kind of territorial limits, some clearly stated claim to time and space that allows him to breathe and to refresh himself. No relationship can survive an over-abundance of closeness.

Misunderstandings about space can be very pain-ful. Some people become very upset when they are told that their partner needs to be alone. They take the matter personally. Sometimes they feel hurt because they see their partner's desire for space as a breaking away, or as a threat. Even if they are right, there is little they can do to hold the partner back. The best way to prevent a rela-tionship from destroying itself over the question of space is to allow each partner to have the space he needs. If living space is not allowed, the rela-tionship is doomed anyhow.

Everyone needs time for woolgathering, resting, for avoiding the sound of another human voice or just for paying attention to the counsel of one's inner thoughts and feelings. Everyone needs to remain in touch with the quiet parts of their thoughts that do not easily find their way into consciousness amid the noisy stresses of daily life.

Some thoughts, some of the best thoughts, require a period of time before they seem willing to appear. It is difficult to keep a tender thought about a person who is continually at your heels during the day, asking you what the matter is or if you feel all right or if he said something that upset you.

To keep a person from the space that allows him to hear his own thoughts is sometimes to keep him from the most important part of himself.

In forming a relationship two people decide to live together and share life as it comes and to offer each other their affection, advice and support in meeting the disappointments and hardships that come to everyone. The capacity to give grows in each partner with understanding, sharing and accepting and with the space to grow.

A relationship means to try to solve the differences between two people instead of running away from them or pretending that they are unimportant without really accepting the other person's right to be different.

A relationship means to try together.

Chapter Four

A HUMAN AGREEMENT

A RELATIONSHIP without an agreement is adrift and takes its shape from what fate happens to throw in its way. In many relationships whatever agreement exists is unspoken. Most formal agreements are framed in the words of some religious ceremony and may have little meaning to the people trying to follow them.

An agreement should reflect understanding of what the relationship means to both people. Two people can agree to follow their marriage vows and live a life together that has no mutuality and caring if their vows are not taken from their personal needs. An agreement should express the viewpoint from which two people try to work out life's problems together—not life meaning the mysteries of time and space, but meaning the needs of two people growing and developing into something more, something only suggested by each of them apart.

There is no easy way to list the points that should be covered in an agreement to a relationship. The charter of a relationship should reflect the attitudes

61

and wishes, the goals and principles of both partners as they have come to understand themselves and as they now see their place together.

The agreement of a relationship is really nothing more than the decision to make an agreement that reflects who each of you is and seems to be becoming.

In order for an agreement to be valid it must allow for growth. An agreement that allows for growth allows for change in both partners and for change in the relationship and in the agreement itself. An agreement must flow with the relationship. If the relationship is to have life, the agreement must also have life. It should be a living understanding that keeps abreast of the changing feelings and aspirations of both partners.

An agreement should never be alien to the relationship or be imposed upon it but derived from it. Whenever an agreement no longer reflects the needs of one person in the relationship, the agreement becomes seriously weakened. If the agreement is not brought up to date but the old guidelines are insisted upon, the stability of the relationship is threatened; for in order to maintain the relationship the partner whose needs have changed is either forced to deny his new needs, which may be impossible, or to lie to his partner.

A great deal changes as we grow, more than we suspected when we were younger and more than we can remember when we get older. As we become adults we strive to find ourselves, set up relationships in families, homes and careers. Still, few of us begin to know who we really are or what it is we really want to become until we reach our late twenties. This does not mean that we don't choose a job, career or mate well before that time. Many of us do. Many of us also end up later feeling trapped and limited by our youthful judgment. Often we wish we had taken more time to make up our minds and had the opportunity to discover what we really liked best and to find out who we were and what our talents were. Too many of us gave up the option to live our lives to their fullest potentials, very high stakes indeed, when the game and we were young.

Obviously many people have made painful mistakes in making their life decisions. Some have chosen well, of course, but the large majority of marriage and career choices don't seem all that suitable to most people's needs and potential. Most people only begin to solve the problems of their lives after they have made their biggest and sometimes their worst decisions. But generally they postpone dealing with their needs. They may try to learn to live with their old choices or wait for all their kids to be in school or get out of school. They may be saving for the day when they think they have enough money to do what they really want to do or they may wait for retirement to put an end to a job they hate. Unfortunately, the day they yearn for seldom arrives in time.

The fact that some people do succeed in working out a life that offers them a sense of purpose and reward is probably more of a tribute to their flexibility and their wish to be happy than to their foresight.

These same people might be happier today had they waited a little longer to discover more about themselves and what they wanted in life and from their partner. They could have avoided much of the frustration of feeling trapped and the worry over making a mistake so early in their lives.

A relationship should be an extension of ourselves, where we can try to become the person we want to become. It should not be a dead end where we merely grow old or try to hide from reality.

Any agreement in a relationship should grow to fit both partners. From time to time at regular intervals the agreement should be redefined from the very beginning to fit the partners' changing needs. This idea may be frightening to some people who may have used their relationship as a way of avoiding personal growth, for they fear that, given the opportunity to state what he really wants, their partner will jump at the chance to run from them.

If your partner is looking for an excuse to run from you, you don't have much of a relationship to start with. All you can lose by redefining your agreement is your pretenses. Too much valuable energy that could be better used in positive ways in the relationship is wasted in maintaining pretenses that both parties may have already outgrown but have not yet admitted to.

It might be helpful to set aside a few days or a weekend and go away, just the two of you, to some quiet place where you will not be interrupted by the pressure of daily events. There you should share your thoughts and try to understand where each of you is in life, where you want to be and where you think you are going. Any agreement you reach should come from an understanding of each other's feelings and goals. The agreement should cover everything that you think is important to your relationship and to yourselves as individuals. It may not be possible to decide every point. Some compromises take years to work out. Others are not possible at all. A good agreement does not try to change reality but provides for adjusting to the truth as it is and as it changes.

No agreement can make two people be good to each other. You have to want an agreement to work to make it work. Without that good faith and mutual understanding no agreement, no matter how well designed or how complete, can ever work.

People, times and circumstances all change and so any agreement between two people involving their feelings must be worked out anew each year and be brought up to date—perhaps on the anniversary of the original, or sooner if either partner wishes.

A relationship has no rights. Only the people in it do.

Neither partner is obligated to a relationship, only to be true to his feelings and honest with the other person. Neither partner gives up any of his individual rights in making an agreement.

In this way an agreement between two people develops so that it comes to mean what two people agree it should come to mean, and that is the only meaning it should have.

Before forming an agreement you must know what you want out of the relationship and what you want for yourself. If you are concerned about a particular issue in your relationship you must make it part of the agreement. This means you have to think about yourself and your needs. It is best to do this alone before you begin to discuss the terms of the agreement with your partner.

It is difficult to reach an agreement that will work for you if you don't know what rights and needs you want the agreement to reflect. Reconsider your individual rights and needs. Accept them as your own.

Allow yourself time to think about yourself. Write down both what you want and need from your relationship with the other person and what you want out of life. After you have a list go over it carefully, asking yourself about each item. How much does this mean to me? Do I really need this? How long have I wanted this? Why haven't I gotten this before?

Your partner should also be making a list and thinking about it in the same way. When you finally discuss your lists together, don't rush or pretend to understand something you do not. Don't allow your partner to pretend for the sake of pride that something is unimportant to him when you know differently. Each of you must look out for the other's rights as well as your own.

Your discussion should try to bring out into the open each of your needs, wishes and goals for yourself and for the relationship. The purpose of talking together is to allow both of you to support the goals and opinions that you both share and agree upon and by so doing redefine your common ground. You should also become aware of your differences and try to understand and if possible settle them. It is useless attempting to settle a problem between two people when only one person is really interested in trying. Going along with a partner insincerely just to avoid conflict is both undermining and cruel and erodes the last ties of trust and understanding.

Caring less than this, not wanting to discuss matters openly and frankly or admit faults and share goals, is only playing at living together. A relationship that doesn't examine itself is make-believe and only works by chance or when both partners close their eyes to each other's faults. If your relationship seems like this, ask yourself what you are hiding from and why you want to live your life like this.

Making such an agreement may sound frightening, but when it is made through love it can be very freeing. A loving agreement makes living together more harmonious not merely through sharing the same space and time together but also by offering a way to help each of you to become the person you want to be. The alternative is to wonder in angry, sullen silence if the other person is holding you back.

You made me special
When you loved me.
What doubts I had about myself
Suddenly seemed
Only silly misconceptions.
I didn't know what was important before.

You gave an order to my being
And I found a reason and strength to grow.

An agreement should indicate how the relationship will function and what responsibilities and obligations each party owes to it and to themselves. There are always conflicts.

Each relationship must have as broad goals:

The continued growth and development of both partners as individuals;

The equal sharing of responsibilities that tend to get in the way of growth and to restrict personal freedom;

And, finally, helping both partners assume and exercise their rights as they see fit to do so.

This means that the care of children is not exclusively a woman's job and that men have an obligation that is equally as great. Two people should agree not to have children until they have agreed on the way in which their children's needs will be met and their own rights preserved.

This also means that merely because one is a man he is not obligated to go out and work nor because one is a woman she must stay home. As often as not the woman is more intelligent, better educated and trained and needs equally as much to participate in the world beyond the confines of a home. There is nothing especially wonderful about having a spotless home and a cluttered or empty mind.

This means that housework, cooking and shopping can be the man's work as well as the woman's. Because tradition has assigned different roles in the past does not mean that they are right for today. Some men need to be protected from stress and some women need to be in open, aggressive competition in the world. The roles each person fills in any relationship should be determined by his abilities and needs, not by society's expectations.

No partner should be made to fulfill a role purely out of tradition. When two people live together they should be prepared to do the same chores that they did when they were living alone. The purpose of an agreement is to allow people to do what they prefer to do and do best and to do it by agreement, not coercion.

If a chore is objectionable to both partners, they should take turns doing it or hire someone if they can afford to. But to make someone do a chore he hates and use tradition as an excuse is to invade rights and to create a source of disrupting resentment.

Before any fair agreement can be reached each person must believe that he and his partner are both worthwhile. When one partner feels worthless he undermines the sense of equality between the two. Such a partner tends to yield his rights too easily and in time may come to resent the other partner for taking advantage of him.

If your partner is unable to stand up for his own rights, it is best to give him the rights you would want for yourself if you were in his situation, no more and no less. Even though you will probably be wrong as often as you are right, at least you will not be usurping your partner's rights under the pretext that he yielded them to you! Later, when your partner feels better about himself, those rights can be discussed again.

People should decide to live together because living together fulfills some of their basic needs more completely. Hopefully in each relationship there are certain needs that are not present in any other relationship but that are generated specifically by the specialness of the other partner.

Knowing that your partner sees your specialness and appreciates it can be the difference between being understood and being alone.

For many people sexual fidelity is not a reasonable standard for defining a relationship. Most sexual encounters that do develop outside a relationship are casual, the product of chance, loneliness, separation or curiosity and may have little to do with the other person. Some people, however, always seem to be looking for the excitement of a new relationship, for the special urgency that characterizes all beginnings and especially the discovery of another human being. Some of these people are trying to supplement what they believe is missing in their life. Some are bored. Other people become involved for the sheer excitement and pleasure. Some are in love with love.

That seems to be reality, the way things are, the way they have always been and probably the way they will continue to be. Who is to say whether it is right or not? It simply is. If a relationship between two people becomes a place where both partners wish to restrict their sexual activity for life, it is greatly to their credit that they have been able to do so. Most people reach that stage only after experiencing other realities, other people.

To insist on sexual fidelity is to make a demand most people cannot meet, even if they would agree to enter into a relationship that placed such a demand on them. The opportunities for sexual interaction are everywhere and people are only human. To demand that your partner promise to be true in a way he may not be able to fulfill may make an insecure partner feel better for the time being but it will not have any effect on the other partner's activities and may create a needless sense of betrayal later on.

The best kind of relationship is one where both partners have the right to become sexually involved with anyone they choose, but choose instead to intensify their relationship by limiting it to each other. If a partner believes that his relationship is imprisoning him he may feel pressured to act in a way that proves he is still free. Of course he really isn't free at all no matter what he does if he has to do something just to prove he is.

Just telling your partner that you do not insist on sexual fidelity is a freeing experience for both of you. It is as simple as this: no matter what anyone says, no one who wants to have sexual relations with a person outside his relationship is going to change his mind or curtail his activity merely because it is prohibited by an agreement. If he feels guilty he may even come to resent you for that guilt. By the same reasoning, no person who is planning to remain faithful will suddenly seek out a partner because he has permission. You cannot pass laws regulating feelings.

In a mature relationship both of you should have permission to love whomever you want. The basis of love is that it is freely given. It is controlled only by the strength of shared feelings, not by rules. To set rules that cannot be followed and in fact are never followed is to create unneeded problems, problems that only distort the truth.

When sexual fidelity becomes one of the ways a relationship is defined, sex begins to take on a meaning far beyond its true worth. Sex becomes invested with so much importance that the other parts of a relationship can suffer unnecessarily.

This is particularly true when a sexual problem arises. In a good relationship sex plays a relatively small part. However, when sex is a problem it seems like a very big problem because it carries with it a physiological urgency which can only add to the desperateness of other unfulfilled needs. Allowing sexual fidelity to become a defining limit of a relationship is like saying, "If you care about me, you are not permitted to care about anyone else." That statement does not reflect human nature. Since most people have some sexual feelings for others, whether they are aware of them or not, most people forced into such an agreement will have conflicting feelings.

Allowing partners to have sexual relations with other people is not going to make anyone unfaithful who wouldn't be anyway, and prohibiting sexual relations with other people isn't going to stop anyone who really wants to.

The real question is: What is infidelity?

Infidelity is acting on the belief that the other person is no longer special to you. No one can be special to another person in every way, but, when a person no longer fulfills the special needs of another as he originally did and that other person looks elsewhere to fulfill those needs, the relationship is changed. The partner who seeks fulfillment of those special unmet needs threatens the basis for the relationship itself. Perhaps the needs can no longer be met, perhaps it is only a temporary loss, but, whatever its basis, the act of looking elsewhere says "You are not able to fulfill me." The relationship is in serious trouble.

A human agreement should be based on trust rooted in a history of sharing and fulfilling each other's needs, most of which are at least as important as sexual needs. People, women especially, seldom leave a partner for sex alone. When people do leave it is usually for understanding, for the need to share something special—for love. When a person in a relationship that forbids sexual freedom does break away, the pull to the outside can be much greater than it is for someone whose former relationship allowed it. What's more, it is much more difficult for such a person to understand the conflicting feelings that inevitably develop. People who are placed in this confusion tend to make foolish mistakes and confuse love and sex the way their old relationship tended to.

One spouse discovering the other's infidelity may become blind with anger at the sexual reality and completely miss the point, that it was not sex that caused the infidelity but a lack of tenderness and a loss of meaning in the relationship. The partner misses the point of the act of infidelity just as he missed the point of the relationship.

You cannot control the affections of another person. You cannot make certain someone else will always love you. The best you can do is to help understand each other's feelings by permitting all feelings to be expressed; to trust the other person's intent; and, as graciously as each of you is capable of, to make allowances for the frailties that are part of being human and that no law, no rule, no set of agreements ever can hope to control.

When you try to control another person's fidelity, you are in effect telling that person that you do not trust him, that you do not value his love for you and that you believe you own his affections.

Puritanical sexual ethics were not so much pure as they were debasing. They were an expression of the unnatural belief that somehow feelings of love were bad and needed to be rigidly controlled. The guilt this created made it difficult for people to examine their feelings and actions freely and to come to terms with themselves as they actually were without worrying about falling short of unnatural standards that few could meet and most were afraid to discuss. Puritanical sexual ethics made hypocrites of everyone.

Being free to love does not mean that you have the right to make the other person unhappy by mishandling your feelings or being carelessly indiscreet should you decide to fulfill that right. Respect for the other person's feeling must always be your first consideration if you seek alliances elsewhere.

If you hurt your partner by such an act it is very likely an act of anger. People who get involved sexually and end up hurting their partner are often simply angry people using the most painful weapon they know even if they protest that they had no control over the situation. A person who has a sexually free relationship is less likely to use an outside sexual encounter to hurt his partner. A sexual encounter used in this way can be one of the cruelest things you can do, for it not only says "I am angry" but also "You are worthless."

Ideally, sexual fidelity in a relationship should develop not by agreement but by choice. When a partner demands sexual exclusivity in a relationship he must bear the burden of providing sexual fulfillment.

To be loved completely is to be loved without the pretense that you are something you are not. If either partner feels that he must live in fear of being found out for a sexual encounter, the relationship suffers. It would be much better if it were all in the open and accepted. When both parties accept each other as human and fallible they can work out their differences without pretending they are perfect and can learn to accept the things they can't change.

One of the most appealing aspects of a new relationship is its newness itself. No matter who you are or how deep your love for another person, certain aspects of your relationship change in time. Preserving a feeling of newness, a sense of discovery in the other is important to any relationship, whether two people are just starting to live together or have done so for fifty years.

To preserve this feeling of newness a relationship should to the fullest extent possible allow partners the freedom to grow and become whatever they would have become if they were not living together. This goal is never totally possible, but some parts of it always can be reached. Just knowing one is free to try to fulfill oneself makes a great deal of difference in a relationship. It is the difference between feeling free and feeling like someone's property. Encouraging each other to reach this goal of mutual freedom should become the basic act of faith shared by two people living together, and the sharing of it becomes the relationship itself.

A relationship is successful if it allows each partner to continue growing into a new person with whom the other can continually fall in love.

In this way the excitement of discovering your old selves only gives way to discovering your new ones.

Each party needs to understand what the relationship means to the other so he can judge how important any particular issue is to the other person. If you don't know what the relationship means to the other person, you make decisions only by chance and continually run a risk of hurting each other.

Each person should be treated as the person he is, not as a symbol of the past or a hope for the future. Whenever one partner has strong feelings about anything they should be shared. Each party deserves an explanation, and even if wrong deserves to be heard. Feelings should not be used as a weapon against each other, withheld for punishment or lavished as a reward. Doing so only cheapens a relationship by giving a market value to emotions.

The only acceptable value to set on emotions is how much they mean to each of you.

The way money is used in a relationship should be determined by mutually agreed-upon goals. Money should not be used to punish or reward. Each partner needs to have some money he is not obligated to account for and each should have an equal voice in the managing of finances. While it may not always be possible, each partner should also contribute to the support of the household, not just out of need but to preserve financial as well as personal independence and dignity.

The territorial limits of each person in a relationship must be respected. Some things must be allowed to be kept private without continuous demands to prove one's innocence.

This means that each party's belongings are free from being searched. Phone calls are private and do not need to be shared. Mail is private.

Each partner has the right to have his own friends.

Each partner has the right to live a part of his own life without making it accountable to the other person.

These rights suggest certain responsibilities. The partners agree to try to make the relationship work. Each partner agrees to try to take care of the other when he is down or hurt without pointing out how much he is sacrificing to do so.

Each partner should agree to treat the other with the same courtesy and consideration he would a stranger. The respect underlying the courtesy should not be relaxed even if the manner of relating is.

Occasional lapses in behavior and attitudes are not always cataclysmic events that signal the end of a relationship. They may only be part of the natural cycle of ups and downs common to all human behavior.

No relationship continues with the same intensity with which it began. Neither party should draw any conclusions from these changes in intensity unless there are good reasons for doing so. One should take courage and joy from the high points in a relationship and use these positive feelings to work out the problems that occur at the low points. From time to time one partner may be called on to perform well beyond his share, such as when the other is sick, under intense pressure or is unable for other reasons to cope with the regular responsibilities he normally carries out. When that happens the active partner should accept his burden with good cheer and not make the other feel guilty because he is being given to.

Neither partner should take advantage of the good-naturedness of the other or his willingness to do more than his usual share of work. When a partner does offer to do more than his share it is usually a momentary expression of goodwill or affection and should be viewed as such, without any other expectation.

Because two people who live together know a great deal about each other and can often see each other's faults more clearly than other people, it is very tempting to be critical when one falls short. Whatever criticisms are to be made should be offered after the disrupting situation has settled down, when both parties are better able to gain perspective to listen and to profit from a discussion.

Two partners should try
To be honest without being vicious
To be open without being undermining
To be mutual without invading the other's privacy
To be trusting without being blind
To be respectful without idolizing

To share without controlling
To love without possessing.

To possess someone you love is to change him, to make that person less himself. Possessing causes resentment and nurtures the weakest part of the other person, the dependent part, the part most unsure to be itself, the part that wants to change and grow the most.

An agreement should offer a love that gives strength and allows both partners to be free.

Chapter Five

CONFLICTS

So it's come to this.
We're fighting again.
Only this time
I really don't know why,
That is, I can't remember
Anything specific.
I'm just tired of hurting
And being hurt.

Maybe we have to let each other be something else
Besides being in love all the time.

Conflicts are everywhere in a relationship. Conflicts in themselves are not so important. Most are trivial, little things. It is how conflicts are used that is important. Conflicts are used as ammunition.

For example, people make a big point about their eating habits, refuse to eat the other's favorite food or to compromise when eating out. People come late or aren't hungry at mealtime. They aren't just fighting over food. Food is only the excuse.

Some people love sports. Others loathe them and resist any effort to get them to move. They worry they will fall short and don't want to be judged failures. Sports isn't the problem.

One partner goes to bed at ten, the other stays up late every night. One partner is always ready to go out, the other is always too tired. Each somehow manages to disappoint the other, to let him down. There are differences in taste—Beethoven versus the Beatles, loud versus soft, antique versus modern, conservative versus flamboyant. The differences only matter when something else is wrong.

There are differences over politics, but you probably bring up politics because you can't think of anything safer to fight about.

There are differences over neatness. Some people could live in a pig pen and not notice the difference. Others go about picking up after people as a way of life. Each complains that the other is being unfair; but they mostly complain because something else is wrong.

When conflicts appear, don't be misled. Most conflicts between people exist long before they are pointed out. Try to discover what is happening between you and the other person that suddenly makes the conflict seem so important. Although many conflicts over taste and style may not go away, it is still possible to uncover the emotion that is using the conflict as the means of expressing itself.

When you solve the problem beneath your disagreement, you'll probably still disagree over food, exercise, habits and tidiness, but it won't matter nearly as much.

Conflict is the language of anger.

There isn't much more I can say
I've told you how I felt
How I didn't mean it
How you misunderstood.
What we are, we are.
And what we can be we'll try.

But let's not hate each other for what we're not.
The day's too pretty and we could love again.

All people who live together fight from time to time. Most fights result from anger that has gotten out of control. Certainly in living with another person you should be able to express all your feelings. Everyone gets angry now and then, and it is not good to hold anger inside. Doing so only allows anger to grow until it surfaces, blown out of proportion, and is expressed in all the wrong places. Holding anger inside also uses up your precious energy, leaving less for expressing positive feelings.

People generally get angry when their feelings are hurt. When people allow their anger to grow without expressing it, they often begin to feel guilty over the anger, and too much guilt leads to feelings of worthlessness and depression.

Although everyone fights, few people know how to have a good argument, an argument that clears the air and makes it less likely a future argument will take place on the same subject.

Some thoughts to consider about arguing:

Try not to start an argument without knowing what it is you are angry about. Arguing for the sake of arguing only makes you seem ridiculous and makes it very difficult to take you seriously.

Before you decide to have an argument think about what you really want to accomplish. Do you just want to let your feelings out, or is there a point you are trying to make? What is it? Do you really understand what you are talking about? Is there another, more direct way to get your point across?

If you argue, try to pick a time and place where you can say what you like without embarrassing the other person. Make the same allowances for his comfort in arguing back. If you set the scene completely to your advantage the other person will know it and will attack you for your unfairness, even if he is unaware he is doing so.

Unless you are planning to pack up and leave immediately afterward you should begin a discussion of differences with the intention of resolving them and making up. Plan for coffee, a walk or some activity together afterward.

Try not to play on the other person's guilt. Don't for example, suddenly run out of the house without telling the other person where you are going when you are getting the worst of the argument. It's not only a matter of being considerate. No one likes to think he has driven another person out of the house, and he will resent you for making him worry about you. Worst of all, you make your argument seem weaker by appearing impulsive and in poor control of yourself. As a result the other person will feel freer to reject your argument and will attach less value to what you are saying.

If during the argument you feel overwhelmed or overpowered by the other person, just say so and ask for the courtesy of speaking your mind with-

out being interrupted. If you feel intimidated tell
the other person. In other relationships it may
be permissible to overpower people, but not between people who are living together. That relationship is supposed to be between equals.

Allow for time to talk and settle differences. Try
not to begin an argument at bedtime, just before
you turn the lights off. This will only make the
two of you more argumentative. Don't fight in
the dark. It is important to see the face of the
person you are arguing with. You learn a great
deal about what a person really means by watch-
ing his facial expressions and how he moves his
body.

Arguing in the dark decreases the amount of feed-
back you'll get. You might miss the most important part of the other person's response. Also,
people tend to be tired and irritable late at night.
You'll both lose sleep, which will only make the
two of you more tired and even more irritable
in the morning.

It is always a good idea to use the other person's
first name frequently during any conversation, but
especially when two people are arguing. When you
call the other person by name it makes the moment a little more real and makes it a little harder
to project your distortions and dissatisfactions

with yourself onto the other. Using first names makes everyone act more humanely toward each other.

Don't argue for the sake of getting attention. Think about what you really want to say and tell the other person in words as simple and clear as possible. Once you have made your point, wait for a response.

When you listen to the other person, see if you can understand what he wants and why he wants it. If you can understand his needs you will understand his actions better.

It is sometimes helpful for two partners to correspond by mail over their disagreements, especially when a particular conflict is so painful that any discussion may lead to arguments that are unproductive and only worsen things. Before doing so, both ought to agree they will only discuss the subject by mail until they agree otherwise. This allows time between responses to think over arguments more carefully, to re-examine positions and to hear what the other person is really saying. Corresponding by letter is a good way to establish and maintain contact with the friendly side of your partner or to say something special that you think deserves to be put in writing and is easier to write than to say in person. And, remember, you can always rip up a letter you have second thoughts about much more easily than you can take back a spoken word.

Is anger coming from somewhere you can't recognize? If you have listened to a person make the same point over and over but still don't understand why he is so angry, ask him if it is possible he might be angry at something else, perhaps a hurt he has not been able to talk about that still eats away inside of him.

People frequently disagree over the facts. One person may not want to see reality as it is because it is too frightening and so he distorts it. From time to time everyone distorts. We all tend to believe what supports our side of the question and doubt what weakens it. When we are under stress we tend to believe what we need to believe. Sometimes arguments get lost in trying to determine whose view of the facts is correct. Both are usually partly wrong, and for one to admit that he is wrong is to run the risk of admitting that the other is right. Putting someone in a position like this is always fruitless. It would be better to begin by admitting the possibility that both of you are wrong.

Some people simply refuse to admit they are wrong. It usually turns out that such rigid people are neither self-confident nor strong but rather frightened and holding on for dear life. It's no use telling such a person that everyone makes mistakes and no one is perfect.

He'll probably think you're starting a confession. Most of us eventually stop trying to reason with people like this and give up on the idea of ever really being close to them.

People who believe they are right all the time can only become involved in a superficial emotional relationship because they can't risk sharing feelings openly. Their partners usually end up looking elsewhere for fulfillment unless they happen to share the same distorted version of reality. Most of the time people simply humor rigid people.

If no one is ever completely right, no one is ever completely wrong. And what is right may change. A correct decision made today may turn out to be exactly wrong in the future.

The point of all discussions, of all arguments should be to try to discover a more complete sense of the truth. Not such weighty truth as what is the origin of the universe, or why good often goes unrewarded and evil sometimes unpunished, but rather the honest appraisal that makes known the true meaning of the feelings two people have about each other. Such truth derives from more than one perspective, from the viewpoints of each. Each viewpoint by itself reveals at best incomplete truths because it suffers from self-serving and self-preserving distortions. Each one's viewpoint needs to be verified and corrected by sharing it with the other. An argument ought to be the attempt of two people to resolve the distortions that exist between them and obscure their perception of the truth.

Truth discovered and defined by this hard work is liberating and dependable. It is a relief not to have to discover the truth of everything by oneself.

As each person grows he has experiences that alter his perception of himself and modify his need to protect his self-image by distorting truth.

Sometimes an overwhelming sudden loss or an unexpected turn of good luck allows us to take a less defensive position and to yield a position without resistance that only the day before we were prepared to defend at any cost.

Our needs distort our perceptions. Our fear limits our ability to understand the importance of the events in our lives.

Two people should allow confrontations to take place as painlessly as possible in order to realign both partners' sense of reality, to share the meaning of each other's view of the world, to lay the groundwork for growth within a framework of trust, and to permit both to say "I was wrong" without fear of being laughed at or taken advantage of.

> *Of course I hurt*
> *It always hurts*
> *When the truth*
> *Catches me by surprise*
> *And makes me see*
> *The part of me*
> *I don't want to see*
> *But need to see*
> *And needed to be shown.*

No one is honest all the time. We tell most of our lies not to deceive others but to protect ourselves from a truth we may not yet be ready to accept, such as pretending not to want something we really want very much or from a view of our weaknesses, imperfections and vulnerabilities we have never seen before and are afraid to face. It takes a lot of love for two people to be honest, a feeling of acceptance from the other and the knowledge that one will not be rejected for admitting one's errors.

To be accepted after admitting you were wrong
is the good result of having an argument.

Thank you
For not pushing me away
When I reached over to touch you
And to be friends again.
I never hurt anyone
As much as I hurt you
Or was ever hurt so deeply
By anyone else

Or ever found anyone who was as happy as I
To make up and risk being hurt again.

No one yields a point unless he feels he can adopt
another position without fear. When a person has
no alternative but to surrender ignominiously, he
will fight to the last, supporting ideas he may not
even believe in, refusing to yield because the issue
has now become his honor.

To make another person grovel for forgiveness
after proving him wrong is probably at least as
hostile as the other person's original offense. Now
the roles are reversed. The aggressor becomes the
victim and the scene is set for a future confrontation. The new victim feels he has a score to settle
and begins immediately to build his defenses for
the next fight.

Arguments badly solved seek repetition. An argument without the possibility of forgiveness and acceptance is not really an argument but an expression of vengeance.

If you are seeking vengeance, recognize it before it destroys you. Vengeance has a way of becoming more malicious than the events that lead up to it. The anger we harbor in silence seethes and grows, pushing our nobler dispositions to the side, recruiting our creative energies to form consuming fantasies of destruction and rage.

No one really enjoys being angry and few people feel entirely comfortable expressing angry feelings. But angry feelings should be let out and shared with the person who caused them as soon as possible. The anger is relatively small then and more easily managed. Moreover your hurt is still fresh and makes your anger seem reasonable, both to you and the other person. The best way to express your feelings is to begin by saying "You hurt me" or "You hurt my feelings."

If the other person cares, just knowing he hurt you should be almost enough to get him to set matters straight. If he doesn't care, you have a problem no argument can settle. If the other person won't allow you to express your feelings, you should ask yourself if your relationship is the right one for you and you should tell the other person that you are asking yourself the question. Eventually you should act as your feelings, carefully considered, dictate.

Chapter Six

GOALS

THERE is nothing as exciting or as wonderful as choosing a difficult goal, working hard and succeeding. It's not the success that is so important but the process of growth, of becoming more than one set out to be and in the bargain discovering a better part of yourself.

No two relationships share the same goals. A relationship is really an arrangement between two people to reach goals they have mutually agreed upon and promise to redefine together.

Even so, when they function at their very best, most relationships seem headed in the same direction—toward being open, honest, trusting and developing mutual respect.

Goals are only possibilities. Nothing is for certain.

The most painful part about a setback is not that events did not turn out the way we wanted but that we may end up doubting our ability to succeed. No one is good at everything and most people don't know how hard they can try until they are tested. Setbacks point out weaknesses to be corrected. When the stakes are relatively low we get a chance to see how things can go wrong so that we can avoid making more costly mistakes in the future.

Generally, if our confidence is not destroyed, we learn more from failures than successes. Failures teach us resolve to overcome. They make goals clearer, more immediate. At best our failures provide us with an enemy to conquer. That enemy is mostly ourselves. In learning to prevail over weaknesses the greatest human achievements have been made.

The best kind of person sees in every other a small part of himself that he loves. Nations, races and religions seem petty categories, an artificial separation of people, all of whom he only regards as human.

We are all part of the same miracle.

The miracle is life itself.

To share life with another person and to accept each other with ever deepening understanding is the highest goal of living with another person.

Chapter Seven

VARIOUS THINGS
INCLUDING

Little Things
Numbers
What Is Real
Religion
Loving Sex
Sharing Losses
The Liberation of Women

Little Things

It's not only the big things that strain a relation-
ship.
Little things can pull two people apart.
Like hogging the bathroom.
Coming home late again without calling.
Not respecting a closed door by knocking first.
Forgetting to say thank you after someone goes
out of his way for you.
Not noticing when someone shows they care.
It's the little things that are important.
Like saying hello and good-bye warmly and mean-
ing it.
Kissing goodnight
Trying to be friendly
Smiling and laughing together
Taking the time to ask "How was your day?"
Listening to the reply,
And enjoying the good feeling of knowing
That someone else wants to listen to what you
have to say.

Having a place you can go to be accepted
And have that be your own home.

Numbers

Everyone does a number some of the time.
Doing a number is acting in a way that isn't you,
Putting on airs
Pretending to be involved when you don't care at
    all
Pretending not to care when you care a great deal.
Doing a number is creating an impression
Without knowing why most of the time
Except maybe you're a little afraid.
The difference between doing a number and not
    doing a number
Is like being before an audience and not.
People who do numbers are trying too hard to be
    something.
Some people do a number every time they get
    dressed up
Or walk into the theater
Or order a meal in a foreign language.
Doing a number in a relationship makes it less
    real
Puts feelings into action without understanding
    them first
And only makes two people seem further apart.
You must both help each other become the per-
    sons you already are.

You don't have to try
You just have to be.

What Is Real

Almost everything we see is an illusion. Because
it is an illusion does not mean it is not really there.
Look around you. The form that manufactured
things have is not their own but the invention
of someone who created the idea for their shape
or use.

All of our tools, art and industry are inventions
that were created from nothing but the need to
create, to fill in an empty space. We have filled
the world with our creations, tamed the animals,
paved the meadows, filled the sky with smoke and
the eyes of many people with tears.

All this we created from nothing, from an idea
that was not real, just a thought in someone's
mind.

From such ideas we created a world that we
sometimes find difficult to live in, a world which
came from us but doesn't always serve us. We
want more and don't know why. What we already
have we do not know how to use to our best advantage. We have not taken the time to discover

if we can create a way of life for each of us that fits each of us.

The world inside ourselves is also an illusion, but when it is shared with another person it becomes more real. When our inner worlds are shared through love there are few illusions, because then feelings become real and there is no need to be anything but ourselves.

Religion

We know nothing of God.
Perhaps God is the life force which exists inside each of us,
The capacity for both good and evil.
Each of us must come to terms with the god within ourselves
And serve it as we see it demands to be served.

For some it is a life of religious ritual and for them that is good.
For others it is a life of devotion to the principles of love for all mankind and that too is good.

We are left here largely on our own, it seems,
To make the best of what we are and have been given,
To try to come to terms with the mystery of our origin

110

And to face an uncertain date in the future
When the life force passes from us.
And to speculate on where it will go.
Each person's perception of the world is his own
    and is colored by the person inside.
Each person's construction of God is a manifesta-
    tion of his needs.
Why should one reject another because he does
    not believe in the same way?
Belief, like hunger, is a matter of need.

Seeking God is only one alternative to being alone
And there are no conversions except as one person
    saves himself.
The rest is ritual, warm and beautiful as it may be.
Ritual takes its meaning from the communion of
    people
Participating in it.

Keeping them as a people
But leaving each person to establish a dialogue
    between
Himself and the life force within
And to devote his life to allowing what is special
    within
To find expression outside himself.

Man without a sense of God is only an animal;
God without man is a force without poetry.

Loving Sex

There is a great deal of talk about sex these days. Much of what has been written seems like the desperate titillating the curious. Most of what has been published on the subject seems more entertaining than helpful, more profitable to the publisher than beneficial to the reader. We live in a time of openness and a growing freedom from censorship, but we should remember that merely because something is published does not mean it is guaranteed to be true. Simply because someone has invented a sexual position he claims will bring two people into the deepest emotional union is no reason to believe that it is suitable to you or your partner or to anyone else. Much of what passes for scientific advice is fantasy lacking both serious thought and common sense.

Making love is supposed to be fun, spontaneous and warm. That is one of the ways continuation of the species is insured. But making love is not always sexual and having sexual relations with another person isn't always love. To the fullest extent possible two people should make love without guilt or obligation and should enjoy each other, being as adventuresome as their imagination and taste permit and as giving as they can be. If they are enjoying each other they are making love correctly.

When a sexual problem exists between two people, it reflects a problem in their relationship more often than a lack of technique. You can learn all the exotic methods, be able to locate every erogenous part of the human anatomy, but if you don't know how to reach your partner with a kind word you might as well spare yourself the effort.

When a relationship is right, two people make love all the time. Making love is to do something kind for the other person. Making love means that you not only care for the other person's feelings as your own but that you act on your caring to make him aware of your love. Making love is the ultimate in thoughtfulness, in considering the other person's feelings.

Sex when it is not related to making love is only a game and a difficult one to play with feeling.

To have an active sexual life without feelings of love is to interact mechanically. Whatever joys one finds in this sort of sexual interaction are transient and not likely to make the participants feel better about themselves, merely temporarily relieved.

The difference between making love and having sex is the difference between sharing feelings and expressing instincts only. Both need to be fulfilled together.

The greatest damage to the feeling of sexual excitement is done by taking sex casually, or using it as a tranquilizer. Everyone does so to some extent. But when lovemaking is taken for granted and becomes essentially a habit the other person becomes devalued and is not seen as a partner in love but as an object for relieving tensions. When this happens lovemaking becomes sex only and the relationship suffers. There is less intimacy when closeness is sacrificed for self-gratification.

The idea of making love is to make the good in a relationship better, more intimate, but not to try to heal differences through sexual relations. That tactic usually backfires.

Sexual relations are only one part of making love. They are also probably a much smaller part than anyone who is having sexual problems in his relationship would ever believe. Such people tend to view sex's importance out of all proportion to reality.

It is a mistake to draw conclusions about the depth of a person's love from sexual performance or to assume that because one lover happens to be more facile he understands better.

The best book for two people to read to improve their love life together is the chronicle of each other's feelings about themselves. If love is there, technique will follow with surprisingly little effort. There is no limit to the invention of nice things you can do for another person.

Sharing Losses

When two people share each other's lives they share the sadnesses as well as the joys. The purpose of two people living together is not merely to make life more happy but to share each other's losses and through that sharing make them lighter.

A loss leaves us empty, sad and hurt. If we don't give our sadness words the loss seems to grow and weighs like a burden on what is good in us. At a time of loss people need to know they are not alone and that someone understands the meaning of what it is that has been taken away. People need to hear a voice sharing their emptiness.

Things taken away
Come back to me now.
Life is so fragile
Like a shadow on the water
Broken by the wind
Irreparable.

I relived all of my old losses
When I heard of yours.

115

When a loss is shared with someone else close both people gain something. The act of sharing a special sadness makes two people closer, and that in itself may be an affirmation of the meaning of life.

Can I do anything
To ease that hurt
That hurt me
When it touched you?
Can I be anything more to you,
Grow to fill your needs,
Offer myself?

I want to say something only time can say
To restore hope when life is taken away.

The Liberation of Women

Finally half of humanity has a chance to be itself, pretenses are dying out, women can be something else besides what anxious men permit them to be. Just as good, just as bad.

Some women have missed the point and have become aggressive and competitive like the worst of men. Women should not become like men. Men should not become like women. All of us need to become more human, accepting, warm and loving, unafraid to feel or to care.

The movement grows daily in magazines, pamphlets and books, in courses and in groups.

Why does it take so much just to be treated decently?

Chapter Eight

WHEN PARTNERS CHANGE

BECAUSE people live, they change.

Agreements made years ago to love, cherish, honor and obey have other meanings now. In a clearer light time has shown many dreams to be merely dreams. So much was hoped for the future, and some days it feels as though the only thing the future brought was added years and a limited familiarity with each other's ways and a more or less easy acceptance of each other's limitations.

People grow, relationships change.
Time in a relationship often seems confused.
What is more important—the future, the present or the past, plans and intentions, accomplishments or hopes?
So much goes wrong. So many ideas become memories before they have a chance to become themselves.

People change, relationships grow . . .
And sometimes people grow apart because there

121

is no room left in one partner's vision to grow
together.

*"Why do you want to do this, to become another
    person?*
What was wrong with the way things used to be?
We were both happy then."

"We were just children. It's different now."

"But we were happy."

"We didn't know enough to be unhappy.
Besides we're not children anymore."

*"Why do we discuss this endlessly and never get
    anywhere?*
If you want to be the way you say you need to be
I can't stop you. I guess I'm afraid to try.
I used to believe that I could always grow
And become the person you needed me to be.
But I'm older now
And I'm used to the way the two of us are
And I'm afraid to try to be something
I've only heard about in your dreams."

What do you do when your partner changes and
seems to become another person, different from
the one you knew? When someone's horizons
change, the way he sees the rest of the world
changes too.

When two people have helped each other grow, they have nothing to fear from change. Whatever each becomes is acceptable to the other, just as each accepted whatever the other was lacking before.

Two people need not be equals to each other, just necessary parts of each other's reality.

This is going to be a solo flight.
I'm sorry for that, but it's the only way
I can do
What I have to do just now.
We've done so much together,
Discovered the world,
Found a home for our deepest feelings,
Shared losses, wiped away each other's tears
Now I have found a new part of me that wants to
    grow
I have visions of a better me
Not really that much different.
No one changes just like that,
But enough to make the way our world is
Seem older than I remembered it to be.
Just as soon as I try my wings
I'll come back and teach you how to fly.

Sometimes when people change they outgrow a relationship they thought always would suit them. They discover parts of themselves that no longer seem to fit the way they used to see themselves.

What is the sense of opposing such growth? When someone finds himself he doesn't usually leave behind the person who loves and encourages him.

Encouraging a person to try to find himself is the best way of keeping him and of helping your relationship grow to catch up. Trying to sabotage his plans or withholding your enthusiasm and support is the quickest way to push him away and to prove that you no longer belong together.

When your partner makes a move which fulfills him, it can threaten you if you think you are going to be left behind. Sometimes a relationship does break apart when one partner changes. The surest way to destroy a relationship is for one partner to stand in the way of the other partner's self-fulfillment. If you think about it, that goes against everything a relationship stands for. A partner should be able to rely on the other's love and support to help him grow into the person he feels destined to be. To stand in the way is the same thing as saying, I don't want you to be yourself.

Relationships sometimes do end when one partner changes because the other becomes too frightened by the challenge of growing.

Whenever anyone changes or grows it is only natural for the people close to him to feel threatened, partly because they feel shown up, partly because they are afraid to try and partly because their lives look stagnant by comparison. Everyone seeks his own reason for being, but the answers escape most of us. When someone seems to be on the road to solving the mystery of his own life, our unsolved mysteries suddenly become more urgent and our frustration becomes worse by comparison. We simply feel envious.

It is easy to forget how difficult it is for someone to make a change in himself, to stop pretending and just be himself. The decision to change takes courage and energy and involves making plans and finding the best way to implement them. Putting up with hardship, failure and discouragement is draining and time consuming. When anyone announces that he wants to change, to grow, to become something better, give him all the room he needs.

If he has already made a decision and is serious about it there is very little that can stand in his way; you shouldn't become an unnecessary obstacle.

When one's partner in life offers the most resistance, the person wanting to change not only feels let down but also betrayed. Lack of support from one's partner is a vote of no-confidence from the person who knows more about you than anyone else in the world. This can be one of the most destructive of all acts in a relationship and the one that ultimately causes the breakup.

Most people who try to change aren't as successful as they hoped to be when they were first considering the possibility. The struggle is often hard and disheartening enough to make people change their minds all by themselves without a partner discouraging them. Why risk being a villain unnecessarily?

Generally when a couple joins forces to help one of them change, they both grow and both their roles change. To discourage change is to limit your relationship and to draw a line in the dust past which you refuse to be led. When you do this you force your partner to decide between fulfilling himself and not fulfilling himself. How would you decide?

A relationship that is not committed to growth together is short-lived.

If a relationship works, the roles of the partners constantly change. When roles change unequally some relationships do fail, but that is no reason for not changing or to wear emotional blinders your entire life. Your life is all you have and finding the role that's best for you should be your lifelong task. To deny your partner's right to grow is to question his value as a person and to deny your own.

A person who begins to realize his potential usually becomes more giving, more understanding of himself and the world around him and has less need to pretend that things are what they are not. In short, he becomes more of a person to love.

An attempt to change roles can be frightening. It often fails and it sometimes hurts the people you love. Who can command another person to stop growing, to stop wanting to be everything he has the potential for becoming? Does anyone have the right to say what another person may become?

To say that another person is totally yours is also to say that he cannot be his own. If we do not belong to ourselves we cannot give ourselves to anyone.

You cannot be loved by someone who does not have the right not to love you.

Chapter Nine

FRIENDS

EVEN if you can't be lovers all the time you can still be friends. Friends define friends and friendships define friendships.

When two people share a friendship they share a special identity that only exists when they are together or when they think about each other.

Friendships are more important than anything else we know. To have no friends at all is the worst state of man. To have only one good friend is enough. A friend makes all the difference in the world.

Friends share the same vulnerability. What wounds one wounds the other. Some friends share each other's vulnerability by possessing the same weakness in common. Other friends share by understanding and empathy.

It's not that hard to be a friend.
I've read books
Telling me what friendship

Is all about
In modern terms
Like "trusting" and "getting close"
But I never had a friend before
Who shared a part of me
I'd only loved in secret.

A friendship is a part of another person that lives inside you, a familiar remembered voice that speaks, calms and restores through the memory of having shared a secret bond.

If you weren't my friend
Not much would change really,
I'd still be me.
I'd just spend more time looking
For a part of me
That hasn't been defined yet,
For a person who was a place to go
When I needed to find myself.

The past seems continuously swallowed up by the future. Sweet memories fade, urgent conversations drift into dimness and faces of old friends become dreamy shadows. Part of the past, the best part, can live again when shared between two people who love the same memory.

I guess you are my friend.
I've had friends before
Many of them

FRIENDS

Who told me
They'd stick with me,
Always be there,
But I never had a friend
Who accepted all of me before
Without waiting for something to happen
To make our friendship necessary.

Chapter Ten

WHEN A RELATIONSHIP
GETS INTO TROUBLE

RELATIONSHIPS get into trouble for as many reasons as there are people.

Sometimes they fail because neither partner wishes to compromise or knows how.

Sometimes they fail because the partners no longer value what they have shared and have not permitted each other to share anything new in too long a time. Sometimes they fail because a partner has fallen in love with another person.

They fail through deceit and betrayal, ignorance and rigidity, deception and fear, lack of trust, dishonesty, and because the partners are no longer open with each other.

But all relationships fail because it is too painful to continue the way they are.

When your life with the person you love is going badly it is very difficult to think clearly, to work at your job, to create, to be warm and outgoing, to be courteous to strangers or to have enthusiasm for anything you undertake. So much energy and feeling is tied up in that close bond with another person that when things go badly there it often feels as though the world is falling apart.

And that is exactly the way it should feel, because the world the two of you have built together, the place where you have spent so many hours in each other's accepting trust, the refuge from the world's madness, is being threatened. Part of your life, part of your world may no longer be.

Each person must be his own salvation. The meaning that one person finds in his life should not be totally dependent on another. Each person should still be a world unto himself. In the end, each person validates his own being by becoming what he is. Two people also validate each other through sharing their worlds, and by recognizing, encouraging the other's specialness. In this way they discover facets of themselves that are only present with the other. We do not need another person to tell us what we feel or who we are, but we sometimes need another person to tell us he understands and accepts our feelings.

It is the loss of this uniquely shared reality that threatens us so when a love starts to fall part.

How can you tell when a relationship is in trouble? Most people know the signs well enough and can point to them with ease in other couples but not usually in their own lives until their relationship is already in difficulty.

If you are lonely for a part of yourself you feel forced to keep submerged in the presence of the other person, your relationship is in trouble because you can't be yourself.

If you feel you have to go out all the time to feel better, if you don't feel accepted, if your partner never admits he is wrong, if you notice that you are keeping more and more hidden from him, your relationship is in trouble.

The problems that disrupt are usually old familiar ones the partners have brushed aside in the hope they would go away. Some people avoid talking about each other's shortcomings and faults because they believe it is destructive to the relationship to do so. Unfortunately the opposite is true.

When the honeymoon phase of any relationship is over, and familiarity makes the easy distortions that shield two lovers from each other's imperfections more difficult to maintain, the partners feel disillusioned. Doubts pass through their minds. They wonder if they have made a mistake. Little hurts that had formerly been overlooked because the injured party wanted to give the other the benefit of the doubt to avoid confrontation and maintain the illusion of bliss suddenly seem more important and come to the surface. It can be a sad awakening. Fortunately most couples are still quite young when the honeymoon ends and both parties have their youth and enthusiasm to apply toward finding new solutions and toward growing.

Anyone who still expects to grow is young.

As people grow older and become more familiar with each other, they tend to be more casual about invading each other's emotional territory and taking the other for granted. This happens universally and isn't necessarily bad. Somewhere between invasion of privacy and aloofness is a balance each couple must work out for itself according to each partner's idea of closeness, trusting and sharing. When partners begin to feel that they are losing their identity by being together so intensely, serious troubles begin. Feelings of being trapped alternate with the wish to be free and the fear of being taken for granted.

What makes a person feel taken for granted? Not being listened to, not being cared for, not being touched, held, spoken to lovingly and not being understood or respected. People feel devalued when they must always be the one to give in, when the other person must always be right, when their preferences in food and entertainment are always the ones to be compromised. People feel devalued when their opinion is not sought or when it is not considered to be as important as another's. People feel devalued when someone always seems to be checking their story, when they are cast in the role of scapegoat, when they are yelled at, physically injured or held up to ridicule publicly or privately.

People feel devalued when their partner doesn't treat them as well as he would a neighbor borrowing a tool, or when every discussion becomes an argument that is blamed on them and their past mistakes.

People feel devalued when they are misunderstood, underestimated or when it is assumed that they have no future, no potential for growth and reform, triumph and success.

People feel devalued when they feel unloved.

The first sign that a couple is in trouble is pain. Pain comes from experiencing a loss or an injury. The first pain comes from recognizing that your situation is neither what you want it to be nor what it used to be. You feel pain because you recognize that the relationship and you have both lost something.

What is it that you have lost? Losses especially in the early stages of a relationship's troubles are often difficult to define. Almost everything you can lose in a relationship can be placed in one of three categories: the loss of a person's love, the loss of a feeling of control and the loss of your sense of personal esteem or self-worth. If you feel you have lost something, share that feeling with the other person as soon as you can. Sometimes sharing the sense of loss forms a new bond.

All emotions fluctuate in intensity. Sometimes people feel very much in love with each other for no particular reason. The intensity of love, especially erotic love, varies tremendously. A preoccupation with sexual involvement this week may be replaced by total indifference next. It would be less disruptive if feelings ran a more even and predictable course, but most do not. Both parties have the responsibility of explaining to the other how their feelings fluctuate so as to prevent misunderstandings.

Each person passes through many cycles in his life. No two years in one person's life are alike. Even the seasons come to mean something different to a person as he matures. It is unrealistic to expect that a partner's feelings, no matter how good their intent or how loyal and devoted a love they are based upon, will always remain the same in intensity and meaning. To demand this kind of constancy is to deny the other person's right to live and be influenced by the world around him.

An important step in solving your problems is to talk over the changes that disturb you. Talking is not always easy and the words of one's heart frequently do not become the words of one's tongue. We all soften our complaints to protect others from being hurt or to keep from admitting to ourselves that we are not as happy as we would like to be. It is a painful task to acknowledge to the other person that something is lacking between you.

At first just trying to talk is more important than what you say. You are trying to share your feelings and each time you do you will come closer to saying what you really feel and mean. Don't try to force an answer from the other person or to settle the matter right away. At least you have begun a dialogue that can last as long as the two of you.

Learning to talk together is only the first step. By talking together you affirm that you are both important and that you intend to form a union where both of you are valued as something more than you would be if each of you were living alone.

It is much easier to get into the habit of talking about problems when a relationship is young and still has strong positive feelings to carry it over the rough spots. It is when a relationship is older, when the areas of conflict are much better known and stand out like immovable obstacles, that working out problems becomes more difficult.

We've lived together for years now,
Our children have come and gone,
We didn't do everything we wanted
And we gave up things we wanted very much to do.
It's difficult to say if I still love you.
There were times when I wondered if I ever did
It's hard to say why we ever got together
Or how different life would have been another way.
Even though there is much you still can't give me
I'm so very used to being with you as you are.

Most relationships that are in trouble today have not been in trouble for a few months like some teenager's or a year like some young married couple's.

They have probably been in trouble much longer than that. Some people, mostly married, have had trouble for years—some for decades and some for as long as the two people have made a life together.

Some relationships seem destined to be in trouble before they begin. All relationships have at least one troublesome conflict.

144

People who become involved in a religious marriage should do so because they love the ritual and believe in the creed, not because they need ritual and creed to solidify their union. It never works. The skeptic who does not believe will not let a ritual stand in his way when he wants to leave.

Why should we make so many religious ceremonies hypocrisies? Some people plainly should not have gotten married in the first place and should not have to mock the integrity of a religious ceremony when they want to get out of their marriage. If you wish any ceremony to confer dignity and acceptance, the ceremony must be treated with the same attitude it is expected to invoke.

Too often people have married and feel trapped by ritual and convention. They are afraid to admit that their marriage has been less than they wanted. They hide from the truth and soon neither partner brings up the subject of their disagreements anymore. Too often they sit silently feeling cheated, burdened and stifled. They have given so much for their family, sacrificed their opportunities in life for their children and sometimes, without ever thinking long enough to realize how silly they were to do so, for appearances. The reward of the good and virtuous life is not all that apparent to them. They are miserable. In their hearts, if only they could listen, is a voice that whimpers, "I want

145

to get out." But they just sit waiting for something to happen.

Very little does.

Very little will unless . . .

What do you do about couples like that?
People who aren't young anymore,
Who don't seem to have any options for change left?

When a marriage has run across decades people come to mean more to each other than they may realize. Time has a way of smoothing over disagreements that could never be compromised before. Things that were important then don't seem to be as important now. There is a certain acceptance that comes with the years, a perspective that allows a person to think different kinds of thoughts, thoughts about the world and how it seems to fit together, a perspective that makes life seem less urgent, less frightening. Differences between people seem to matter less.

As people grow older they become like children in their acceptance of each other. Time can make us all childhood friends once more. Just as children share their smallness, and their helplessness in an adult world makes them all brothers, we begin to accept people for their human qualities, their kindness and understanding and for being vulnerable in the same way we are.

Age settles on us like an unwelcome guest telling us disturbing news about ourselves. We put on weight more easily. We have to take better care of ourselves and pay more attention to where we step because it's harder to keep our balance. The eyes are dimmer and complex ideas we used to argue with friends over coffee now elude us. The point of our whole philosophy seems refined to feeling comfortable and remembering our way home again.

Why didn't we know this before, when we still had our brave intent and energy? If only we knew then what the years have taught us, we would not have wasted so much of ourselves trying to conquer the world. Perhaps we would have taken the time to understand who we were to each other and what our life together meant without fighting over what we could not change. Perhaps we would have taken more time to conquer ourselves.

Sometimes it takes the passage of many years for people to realize who they are and what they really need in life. No one can ever be happy until he understands that whatever he becomes he will still be himself and, if he is not happy with himself now, he will not be happy with himself later.

When two people have shared many years together they cannot expect their union to be as fresh or as exciting as it was when it was new. How long does it take for a marriage to lose its newness? Some never feel old. Others seem old before the first anniversary.

A marriage is old when two people feel that there is nothing more to discover together. Since there is always something new to share, most of the marriages that grow old are the ones that allow themselves to grow old.

As long as neither party demands that the other love him, a marriage that has survived years of struggle does not need to be ended because two people are no longer so much in love. Sometimes the best that can be hoped for is to be respected for what you are and simply to be taken in because you belong. Two people who no longer love each other as they used to should admit that fact without blaming each other and just allow each other to be whatever they are.

Sometimes a new kind of love and a deeper friendship blossom when both parties are freed of the obligation to keep up a pretense neither feels comfortable with and both secretly resent. It is very difficult to love again in the same way someone you once loved. Feeling obliged to do so only makes it harder.

Two people who have lived together for years, who have set up a home, a circle of friends, have established family customs and ties. To abandon these because two people no longer love as they once did seems cruel and unnecessary.

When love changes in a marriage it is a difficult time for both partners. Denying that love has changed only makes matters worse. Feelings of sadness are held inside. Lovemaking is undertaken with reluctance, if at all, and the lack of enthusiasm in sharing and being intimate begins to color the rest of the relationship. Both parties already know what is wrong and should admit it.

Why wait for something to happen to bring these problems into the open? To have an affair, be careless and get found out in order to bring the matter to your spouse's attention is unkind, painful, amateurish and less likely to help settle your differences than to create new problems. Unfortunately this is how many married and other couples learn about the other's change in feelings. It is awkward, produces unnecessary guilt and remorse and tends to make people who should know better act like fools.

Wouldn't it be better to say something like, "Our relationship has changed. My feelings aren't the same for you as they used to be and I can tell that your feelings for me aren't the same either. I love you but I love you in a different way and I want to talk with you about how both of us feel."

Why keep feelings like this inside? There's nothing wrong with feelings. Feelings are the truth even if you don't always understand them. What is wrong with admitting that you are both human, that a decade or two of living together can change feelings, that the two of you have changed and need to redefine your relationship to fill both of your needs? Your feelings and needs are what they are. Denying them won't help. Denying will only hurt what is good and still has promise.

Once you have let your feelings out, you will probably discover that there is much more for you to share and build with than you realized. You will probably discover that your feelings for each other are stronger than you imagined. When feelings of resentment and obligation subside, your friendship and even your love may start to grow again. Sometimes all that is needed to fix an ailing relationship is to admit what you feel without pretending to be what you're not or to feel what you don't.

It may take time to admit to feelings of tenderness, especially if one of you insists on playing games or acting overly hurt or tries to play the role of the shocked victim as if you both didn't know what was going on all along. If you both didn't know something was wrong before, how will you be able to tell when things get better?

All you can lose by admitting your feelings is your pain. There may be some pain expressing your feelings for the first few times. But once that is past, once two people know that they have to rebuild their relationship on the feelings that are there, not on what they hoped were there, the pressure is off. All each partner must be at that point is himself. No pretenses, just honest feelings and saying what you mean.

You may have lost the belief that love is forever and never changes or that people are always true to each other, but you may find a new faith simply in trying to do your best, without making excuses or expecting too much. Only by accepting each other for what you are and for what you give, and by learning to take the responsibility for your own happiness without making demands on your partner to take away your emptiness as a person, can two people working as equals begin the task of finding out what their possibilities together are.

Often a relationship becomes disrupted because a new love has taken over the affections and interest of one of the partners. This is especially difficult for the other, who is tormented by the painful realization that his partner is still capable of experiencing the intensity and depth of feeling he has been yearning for in their relationship but has been unable to evoke. It is especially difficult when the new love is of such a different quality that it is more an awakening of new feelings than a simple affair.

The competition is overwhelming and a dangerous threat, especially if the other partner tries to win his mate back by making an expansive or inappropriate show of affection. At best such attempts are embarrassing and appear insincere or staged. What is worse is that the enamored partner is involved in a relationship in which the feelings seem intensely real. It would be best to avoid trying to compete with the new lover. The new lover has too much going for him. You can try your best and not even remotely arouse the feelings the new lover awakens just by being natural. You'll most likely come off second best if you compete.

When something like this happens there are no hard and sure rules to follow and the advice offered here may be difficult for many people to accept. Just try to be your best self. Try to understand if you can.

If you can't understand, keep your temper. If you can't keep your temper, take a vacation. Be as reasonable and as pleasant as possible and offer to participate in the parts of your relationship that still have meaning for you and in which you can become sincerely involved without staging a performance. If you fall short try not to let it get the best of you—you're not supposed to be a saint.

If your relationship has anything left going for it and you permit your partner to feel comfortable with you and enjoy your time and your home together, you are better off than with any other approach.

To make demands or to try and force a showdown by ultimatum is unwise. An ultimatum assumes that you have the right to control another person's feelings or that he has the absolute ability to comply with your ultimatum if he wishes. Both views are mistaken. What the two of you need is time, time to adjust to the new reality. Your feelings have changed and you both need to understand them better. It is of limited value to attempt to restrict the other person's access to what he wants. It also tends to portray yourself as a frightened and vindictive person and only makes your rival's case seem stronger. Sometimes it may be best to separate for a while.

Your case is you. Your strength is your friendship and what you have shared. In so many ways you have become part of each other's reality, life. Do not deny what you are to your partner. Pretending you don't care will only undermine your position further and makes it more difficult for your partner to see you as a person who can fulfill his needs if that is how you still see yourself—which doesn't mean that you forget about your dignity and personal honor. Be flexible, but don't panic.

Leave the door open. For all you know this is a short, painful experience for the two of you but one that may clear away some of the pretense of the years and allow the two of you to relate more honestly and with more real feeling than you ever have before.

You can never go back to the way you were, but if you handle the present difficult situation well it may become the point when your relationship with your partner becomes open and more mature. It may be the point when you both start to grow together again.

If you want to be forgiven, forgive.

Chapter Eleven

MAKING A
NEW COMMITMENT

MAKING a commitment to another person is one of the most important events in anyone's life. In that single act of deciding to make a life together some people have insured their success, others have sealed their failure. Nothing most people do even faintly approaches making a commitment to another person for the impact it will have on their future.

And yet people make commitments without having enough understanding of who they are, what they are doing or what a commitment means.

When people make a commitment too early in life they risk limiting their own growth. Most relationships early in life, no matter how intense they appear to be, are really only experiments in living with another person. Too many people live with another person without having any idea of what doing so entails or what they can expect from their relationship. Not knowing what to expect, they struggle to understand their feelings and those of their partner, they search for meaning in the moment and try to develop goals as the situation evolves.

To subject any relationship to this built-in lack of perspective seems unfair. To expect two young people to understand the nature of a commitment when they do not yet understand themselves seems even more unreasonable.

When two people get married in their teens they often do so to solve an immediate problem that may have nothing to do with becoming the person they have the potential to be, such as wanting to get away from their parents or the fear of going unmarried or not being able to get a job. Not all marriages made at this time of life are failures, of course, but they require two unusually mature people to make them work.

Weak marriages generally occur between people who do not yet understand who they are and who have not developed the skill to see how much their perception of the other person is the product of their imagination and wishful thinking.

To some extent everyone imagines the person he loves to be the person he needs. That distortion in fact shows how infatuation works. If that distortion represents most of what a couple has going for it, the partners are obviously starting off on the wrong foot. To maintain such a distortion throughout a relationship ultimately gets in the way of emotional growth, and young people have a great deal of growing to do. Also, keeping up pretenses may result in a marriage that is forced to become rigid for the purpose of resisting change or avoiding the discovery that one's affections have changed or that a mistake was made in the first place.

The part of love that depends on distortion rapidly becomes weakened by time. Keeping the feelings of the partners fresh is difficult enough to do without being committed to a rigid distortion. A relationship based on distortion never achieves the flexibility needed for the growth of both parties, and makes it all but impossible to feel joy. Joy is real. It is the real fulfillment of real needs, not the offering of substitutes to satisfy an expectation based on a distortion.

The story of most loves is that they change and grow to reflect the circumstances and stresses that affect each of the partners. Two people may be very much in love when they are young. Although that love may not diminish over the years, each partner's idea of what love is may change through his experience in and exposure to the world. As he grows each partner will be forced to confront new parts of himself that he wasn't even aware existed before, let alone had any idea would require fulfillment. A partner may be asked to fulfill a role totally unsuitable to his character when his partner's needs become known. He may grow with the challenge and do admirably or he may not. Many confusing problems of identity in late adolescence are short-lived. To attempt to solve them by making a long-term commitment is like betting your life savings on the first hand of cards you play without any need to do so other than your desire or need to gamble.

Another problem in making a commitment too early in life, especially within the set framework of the conventional marriage, is that the opportunity for personal growth and development is limited by the relative immaturity of both partners and by what they experience within their marriage. Too much of the external world, the advantages that come only from getting to know other people, are missed in the hope that the partners offer all the best possible solutions to each other's needs. That places an unrealistic burden on each for being everything the other needs, and may be neither possible nor in either's best interest as an individual. Why should two potentially valuable but unformed people sacrifice their future for the moment? An early commitment carries at best a hope that the two partners have made the right choice. It is difficult to make the right choice for yourself when you haven't finished becoming who you are. Of course we never finish becoming ourselves but we should at least give ourselves enough time to understand the direction our life seems to be headed in. Take your time. If your choice is right, it will be right in a year. If it's not right in a year, it probably wasn't right before.

When two people make a commitment to form a relationship they should try for a moment to put aside their intense feelings for each other and consider some practical matters that need to be attended to. Each partner should look upon a relationship, whether he is starting a new one or trying to restore an old one, the same way he would look upon a new job.

For example, each partner should discuss his abilities and describe how he sees his future role in the relationship. Both partners should agree on the work requirements involved in maintaining a relationship and household and list the jobs that need to be done. The partners should try to develop a schedule to assign responsibilities, making sure that special preferences and dislikes will be shared equally and in rotation and that neither party is taken advantage of.

Partners should arrange for a regular meeting no less frequent than once a week at some quiet time in order to discuss the past week and to bring up any concerns or questions that have bothered them. This weekly meeting should have certain rules. Each party should agree to listen to the other without interrupting, to be reasonable and fair, to try to be honest and to agree to talk about any feeling or complaint with sincerity.

Each couple should understand that this meeting represents a vital part of the work involved in keeping a relationship open and fresh. Even though some sessions may be dull it is important to have them last at least one hour each week. It sometimes takes a little while to get the conversation going. Be patient. Think of it as an investment. It really is!

Sometimes two people need help in understanding what their needs are, what they are really like or what goals they consider important. Most people do not think in an orderly fashion. They get part of an idea here, part there and several weeks later another part, although now perhaps they can't remember the previous ones that relate to it.

A good method for taking an inventory of your thoughts and feelings is to write them down, any that you feel are important, on a small card. Use a different card for each idea. After a while, when you have a dozen or so, try to place your cards in categories, labeling the cards at the top for easy recognition. If a card doesn't fit into any category set it aside on its own.

162

After several months you should have many categories, including your feelings about yourself, the person you are living with, your personal goals, peeves and pleasures. You will discover that your feelings are more complex than you may have realized and that most feelings have two sides to them—that, for example, your love for the person you live with may also cause you to feel irritation when you feel disappointed by him. Your goals may seem too vague, such as just wanting to be successful, or they may seem too inflexible. Your peeves may suddenly seem petty or you may discover that you have been hiding your real feelings from the other person out of fear. Ideas you may formerly have ignored will begin to seem important to you and you will start to have a more complete understanding of what you really are concerned about. It is very important for you to know what is on your mind most of the time. It is equally important that you be the only one to look at these cards, at least for the time being while you are discovering yourself.

The idea behind all this is that the view we have of ourselves is generally the view at one moment, now. In order to take stock of ourselves we need perspective. Time gives us that distance but it still takes a while to develop understanding. The cards make that process much faster. Keep the cards as uncomplicated and as brief as possible. Just put down what you were thinking and occasionally why, if you can figure it out, and go over the cards every so often.

Anyone who keeps such close watch on his thought process will develop a much clearer picture of himself and his needs and will be better able to say what he is all about. In time, when you understand yourself better, you can present some of your ideas to your partner for discussion at your weekly meeting.

This technique of having meetings, writing idea cards and sharing them is good for couples who are just starting as well as for those who have been together for years and don't know how to make contact with each other again. It allows each partner to maintain a private examination of his relationship and of himself and gives each fresh material to discuss if he so chooses. The cards also help people to be surer of their feelings. They are a kind of concrete evidence of one's emotions. Finally the process itself will frequently initiate a new exciting adventure in discovering new parts of one's self.

Taking stock of your feelings and your relationship in this way and sharing your viewpoint with your partner is of enormous help in keeping the growth process alive and insuring that the two of you keep working together. Without knowing what your goals are it is very difficult for you to tell when you have what you want. If you aren't sure of who you are and what you want you sometimes can't tell when you have what is exactly right for you.

A person who does not know what he wants in life cannot expect to be fulfilled in a relationship with another person except by chance.

In forming a commitment of any kind, either new or renewed, both parties should be committed to developing and preserving honesty, sharing and accepting the truth of their relationship whatever it turns out to be.

Chapter Twelve

LIVING WITH
YOUR FAMILY

THE best of all things is to belong to a family. To come home without fanfare and simply to be let in. To be each other's.

The way our families saw the world influences the way we come to see it. At best we are taught to see life as a challenge, full of wonders, as a place where we can make our mark if we choose to and where we can find ourselves as we are, without having to be anything but ourselves in order to be loved.

You can never leave your first home behind even when it all seems far away. No matter what you do or where you go, you wear the stamp of your beginnings somewhere very close to you, whether you want others to know it or not.

Children and parents become the best things they give each other.

Children have rights in a family just as much as their parents do.

Children have the right to be listened to, to be taken seriously and given an explanation. They have the right to be treated as people in their own right, not merely as someone's child.

Children have the right to be children and should not be expected to behave like complete adults. Although children are incomplete people they still feel and care as much about their feelings as adults do about theirs. Children have the right to be imperfect. They sometimes steal, cheat, lie and take advantage of smaller children. When they do they need to be told it is wrong but not that they are bad for doing so.

Children have the right to spend time with their parents.

Children have the right to assume adult rights as soon as they are able to handle them responsibly, which means without doing harm to themselves or others.

Children have the right to choose their own friends.

Children have the right to become what they want to become. Children learn by example and model. The best way for a parent to influence a child is to act the way he would like the child to act.

If a child is destined to become something his parents object to, his parents' objections only create an unnecessary obstacle for him to overcome later in life. When seeking an important goal later on, the child may be haunted by his parents' unfulfilled wish that he realize their dreams. Although he may someday fulfill his destiny he may feel he is a failure in their eyes for not fulfilling theirs.

Sometimes a child's belief that he can never become the person his parents wanted him to be may erode his self-confidence to the point where he is unable to give the effort required to succeed at the goals he has the ability to reach.

The parents' negative attitude then may become a self-fulfilling prophecy and the child may become a discouraged adult who has difficulty believing in himself or in understanding why his parents could not accept him for what he was. Worst of all he may end up with nothing about himself he can take pride in and not be able to justify a belief that he is worthwhile.

It is a discouraging experience for a child to have his goals misunderstood by his parents. If a parent refuses to think of his child as successful unless he accomplishes the goals the parent approves of, the child may go through life trying desperately to prove that his own conception of himself really exists, that he is something besides what his parents dream for him. Nothing gets in a child's way of being himself more than trying too hard to be what he is not. He will only fail and waste his time covering up for his imperfections and come to wonder if anyone can ever accept him for what he is.

Children have the right to have property of their own. This is the only way children learn to be responsible. A child should not be given property beyond his capability to care for it, because that only invites failure and undermines self-confidence. Although the property is the child's, its use may be limited for a time as punishment by the parent. The limitation should be appropriate, not vindictive.

A child has the right to be treated like himself, not someone's brother or sister, not as someone's child, not as a statistic or a typical ten-year-old, but as a person who feels and hurts and is to be dealt with as an entity in his own right, to be figured out anew and not to be taken for granted or labeled.

Children have a right to have their own feelings and their own reasons for them.

Children have the right to be afraid, to say no, to quit and to cry. They have the right to be com-

172

forted, to be praised, to be adored and to be squeezed for absolutely no good reason except simply happening to be within arm's length.

Children also have the right to try something just for fun, just to see how a role fits or feels without the slightest notion of taking it seriously and without been judged for their performance.

Parents have the right to set limits that should be reasonably arrived at through mutual consent between their children and themselves. This mutual consent is only an ideal, a goal parents and children always fight over. Limits constantly change as children grow and show more responsibility for managing their own lives. Parents are continually weighing their children's capabilities. Children continually test their parents' firmness in setting limits. It is an imperfect system, but, if the ultimate goal is to be reasonable and supportive in helping a child develop independence, it usually works.

Parents have the right to enforce rules. The philosophy behind enforcing rules should be either to insure the child's safety when it is in question or to compensate for a child's inability to make certain decisions in his own behalf. However, the parent must leave enough room for the child to make some mistakes so he can learn from experience and ultimately assume the reins over himself.

Parents have the right to a certain amount of peace and quiet because they put up with a lot and often have no choice in the matter. Parents are older people. Their struggles are not always to their liking or of their own choice. Many of the dreams they had for themselves have not turned out the way they wanted.

The child is hardly at fault for his parents' shortcomings, but it is important for a child to understand that sometimes a parent's job is thankless and even demeaning. Sometimes an employer is arbitrary and unfair. Sometimes friends hurt and people cheat. Sometimes adults are too tired or too frightened to try, too afraid to give up or to change or even to look at themselves in the mirror. Because parents might feel this way at times does not mean that they are failures. And if they share their feelings with their children, the children should give them understanding. Everyone needs some.

In a world beset by exasperating problems and with life getting more and more difficult all the time, one of the few places a person has to be himself is the home he struggles so hard to maintain.

More than likely all parents do things they do not want to do, and whether they are good-natured about it or not isn't the point. Even if they are not able to be the kind of parents one would want in the best of all possible worlds, they are the only parents one has. Wanting one's parents to be something else is no more justifiable than parents wanting their children to be something other than what they are.

In any relationship we need people to wish us well just the way we are and in pursuit of the goals we have chosen for ourselves. We do not want to be judged for our taste and found lacking and be rejected on such grounds. We need to know that we are loved and accepted the way we are without changing to fit other people's preconceived notion of us and their world and their plans for us. No parent has the right to insist that his children be made from the same mold as himself or to demand his child shore up a fallen self-image in hopes of proving by proxy a success that never materialized for the parent. That a parent made a mistake in his own life is lamentable enough without perpetrating the same mistake on his children.

We cannot expect that our relationships with other people, even family, will always remain the same. That is too rigid an expectation. Both parents and children can grow through their changing relationships with each other.

Everyone we meet is growing or changing, no matter how stagnant people happen to feel at any given moment. The process of growth is lifelong. Unfortunately growth for too many people seems to have been limited by their parents' plans for them. Such people are often forced into the wrong adult relationships as they mistakenly try to fulfill parental expectations. Everyone involved suffers because these people are really still children who are not living their own lives.

One of the best things about being a member of a family is that the possibility of being loved, no matter how you change, exists there with the greatest chance for fulfillment. Most parents still love their children even when they have been disappointed by them. It is important for children to understand that some of the disappointment their parents feel for them is often really the parents' disappointment in their own lives. A parent who has pretty much accomplished what he set out to do has little reason to ask his children to make up for what he could not accomplish.

Some parents view *their* children only symbolically, not as people in their own right but only as their children. These are the most difficult parents to live with. Is the child being criticized because he is not acting the way his parents would want him to act or is he doing something that is not in his own best interest? And worse still is the parent comparing him to the way the parent mistakenly remembers himself. Making such distinctions is difficult for the child. It is also difficult for the child to be responsive to his parents' comments. He just isn't sure about their sincerity.

Parents also have rights and their children need to be aware of them. They have the right to expect their rights to be respected in the same way that they recognize their children's rights.

Parents have a right to be treated as people and not to be taken advantage of even when they sometimes seem to be asking for it. They have the right to be treated with the same courtesy and reasonableness as the child would any other adult.

Parents have a right not to be nagged at constantly when they have given a "no" for an answer, providing they have given a reasonable explanation for their action and their child has had a reasonable opportunity to question it. After a while, though, the debate should end.

Unfortunately some parents simply don't care about their families and just don't love their children. Probably they don't even love themselves. That may be the heart of their problem. Having parents like this is a terrible burden for any child and can shadow him all through life. It can even destroy him if he lets it get the best of him. A child of such a parent must learn to stop hating his parent for his shortcomings and to stop

177

hating the parts of himself that remind him of that parent. The child needs to learn to get close to other people, to share a part of himself and to learn how to give and accept being given to—in short, how to love the other parts of himself and accept the good parts of his parents that are also in himself.

Parents have the right to know their children's friends and should be interested enough in their children's friends to know their names and who their families are. It is not enough to know that your children are not associating with people who are negative influences on their lives. It is also important that you are aware of the positive forces affecting your child's life.

A home is a place in time. And no place stays the same after you finally grow up and leave it. No place can ever change as much as the person who grows up there. Streets and buildings may remain much the same no matter who lives there, but people find new places to travel suggested only dimly by the place they grew up.

Parents and children should carry into the world a special confidence and strength from sharing a uniquely intimate time of growth.

Each child should try to see in his parents the children they previously were. Each parent should try to see in his child the adult he seems to be becoming. The child in you should want to play with your children. The adult emerging in your child should find support and companionship in the adult within you.

None of us should feel ashamed of what we were or what we are becoming.

Chapter Thirteen

BREAKING UP

THERE comes a time in some relationships when no matter how sincere the attempt to reconcile the differences or how strong the wish to re-create a part of the past once shared, the struggle becomes so painful that nothing else is felt and the world and all its beauty only add to the discomfort by providing cruel contrast.

Sometimes two people cannot be together. The parts each respects and even loves are not enough to set right the discomfort between them or to change each other so that they can live together again.

Of what use is it to endure a world where one is jealous of lovers strolling on a spring day, where one becomes envious of young people for their freedom and hopefulness and feels cynical about the future? Worse still is a world where to keep our feelings from tormenting us we bury them and pay a price of not being able to feel what we once loved but instead turn inward to a lonely world of self-pity.

It is better by far to admit that a relationship is so fragmented and the effort needed to put it together is so great and requires so much love and caring not presently or soon likely to be available that the relationship should end.

Deciding when a painful union should end is never easy. When things have become this painful it is difficult for two people to talk and the decision drags on and waits to be pushed to the surface by an overt hostile act of one partner today or an equally angry retaliation by the other partner tomorrow.

Why must it end this way? Why can't two people try to make the ending of what has proved bad for both of them become the first positive step in their new lives by treating each other with fairness and a reasonable concern for each other's welfare?

Of what use is it to seek revenge or to perpetrate onto other lives the destruction that has already taken place in the lives of two people?

There is a time for the ending of hostilities, for saying enough, for raising the white flag, for speaking in conciliatory terms, for lowering voices and thinking of doing right by everyone who happens to be involved. There is a time for the two antagonists to part.

It is never easy or simple to do. There are no rules except the rules of decency and respect for the other person's rights, which are the same as your own. It might have been difficult for the two of you to respect each other of late when your relationship was deteriorating, but even if it is a formality to do so now it is essential that both of you respect each other's rights as your relationship ends.

Of what use is it to carry anger around within you and spend a life convincing others you were right and the other party wrong? No one cares to listen anyway and you only make yourself more angry.

Have done with the pain. All of the pain. Do not regret the time you spent together. It is all past.

That past may still shape your future adversely if you do not come to understand in your heart why it went wrong or why your commitments to each other failed. As for the reasons why your relationship failed, you are more in the right than your partner believes and more in the wrong than you admit. Both parties share the failure no matter how bad one partner may have been. Even if you were blameless—highly unlikely—and fulfilled your obligations to their fullest and your partner was the worst sort of person, you are still at fault in forming a commitment before you understood what your partner was like or what you wanted from a relationship with him.

If you had been faultless you would never have become involved in the first place.

When a relationship involving children ends, the children should not be made to feel that it is their fault that the relationship failed. They should be told to the fullest extent possible that *their* lives will remain the same and so will their futures.

Children should not be asked to take sides, used as sounding boards for one parent against the other or used as go-betweens, as objects. Children are still people and still have rights that don't derive from the intactness of their parents' relationship.

The relationship of a parent and a child is ended only by death. Till then it is either good or bad.

When the relationship between them is going badly both parents should try to insulate their children from the raw anger of their hostilities. They should admit to their feelings and explain the state of their marriage but not in the heat of the moment or with the other parent on hand to renew the combat. A child doesn't need to be told very much. A simple statement that his parents

186

aren't getting along well will confirm what he already knows. More details aren't necessary.

A child should not be made to feel that his love for the parent who is to leave is put in jeopardy by the parent he lives with. The child's love for the other parent must be held in the highest reverence, never talked down or undermined. Children are resilient and can pull through almost anything if you allow them to believe in what they need to believe in. You can be honest without dragging your personal opinion into the matter. It doesn't help you to do so and will only hurt your child.

Whatever bitterness and resentment or false hopes that never seemed to materialize you have lived with, they are not yet behind you. The potential to become involved in a relationship that can turn out equally as bad still exists. To pretend that it does not is dangerous and only wishful thinking. But the pain of the past seen in the truest possible perspective will tell you a great deal about yourself and the way you really are. Try to examine your heart and your intentions openly and honestly, accept whatever blame you think you deserve and do not see your faults as fixed but as problems to overcome in the future.

A separation, an end, is also a beginning.

EPILOGUE

NO relationship can provide everything needed for the complete experience of being yourself. Many important answers must come from ourselves, not from another person. The role of another person in our search for ourselves will at times be little more than that of a friendly, accepting bystander. The greatest burdens in our lives will clearly fall upon our own shoulders, not on our relationship with another person.

We must sort out the two and learn what we can expect from our relationship with another person and what we must provide ourselves. Sometimes the problems of life are made more difficult not by seeking what is impossible but by looking in the wrong places for what we need.

Life is a creative process. Each person must find the source of his own creative energy and allow it to flow throughout his life, leaving his imprint on whatever he does. The essence of individual fulfillment is simply to do your best in a way uniquely your own. No relationship can give the same meaning to a person's life that his personal creativity can, nor should it be expected to.

A relationship should also not be measured by how successful it is in warding off feelings of loneliness. That is not its purpose. To insist otherwise is to condemn an apple because it does not taste like a pear or reject a flower because it does not keep you warm.

When two partners hold each other at fault for not making themselves complete as individuals they only deny their own specialness, for no one can make you feel complete but yourself. Rejecting a person because he or she does not make you feel complete or does not resolve feelings of loneliness is self-defeating and results in angry frustration that undermines the relationship and can destroy the person who feels it.

The purpose of life is to celebrate life, to take the life force and make it visible. The purpose of a relationship is to celebrate life together. A relationship should allow both partners to share the specialness of each other, of each other's creations, and to love and support the other person through the difficult periods when it is hard to be one's best self. A relationship should allow both partners full freedom to grow and to become their fullest, most creative selves. To do less is to live less.

A relationship allows you to celebrate another person's view of life and to illuminate the parts of your own life you are unable to see by yourself.

Love is the light of life.